WINE
WIT AND
WISDOM

Maggie Rosen,
Fiona Jerome
and PJ Harris

A Think Book

THE WIT AND WISDOM SERIES

Poker Wit and Wisdom
By Fiona Jerome and Seth Dickson
From nineteenth-century Mississippi river boats to Cockney gambling dens and
.com casinos, *Poker Wit and Wisdom* takes a lingering look at the addictive
world of poker, dealing out all the oddities, quirks and stories along the way.
ISBN 1-84525-004-4

Wine Wit and Wisdom
By Maggie Rosen, Fiona Jerome and PJ Harris
A lingering look at the wonderful world of wine, *Wine Wit and Wisdom* blends
the banquets of Bacchus with the grapes of wrath, and the fruitiest flavours
with the correct way to judge a bouquet.
ISBN 1-84525-003-6

Series Editor
Malcolm Tait

*Penicillin cures, but wine
makes people happy.*

Alexander Fleming

THINK
BOOKS

A Think Book

First published in Great Britain in 2005 by
Think Publishing
The Pall Mall Deposit
124-128 Barlby Road, London W10 6BL
www.think-books.com

Written by Maggie Rosen, Fiona Jerome and PJ Harris
The Wit and Wisdom team: James Collins, Rhiannon Guy, Amanda Hadingue,
Emma Jones, Lou Millward, Matt Packer, Sonja Patel, Mark Searle and Malcolm Tait

ISBN 1-84525-003-6

Printed & bound in Great Britain by William Clowes Ltd, Beccles, Suffolk.
The publishers and authors have made every effort to ensure the accuracy and
currency of the information in Wine Wit and Wisdom. Similarly, every effort has
been made to contact copyright holders. We apologise for any unintentional
errors or omissions. The publisher and authors disclaim any liability, loss, injury
or damage incurred as a consequence, directly or indirectly, of the use and
application of the contents of this book.

Cover image: Steve Lupton/CORBIS

*Wine improves with age – the older
I get, the better I like it.*

Anon

THE AUTHORS WOULD LIKE TO RAISE A TOAST TO:

Stuart George, Neil Beckett, Sara Basra and Wink Lorch

Jeffrey Benson and other members of the UK Circle of Wine Writers

Luis Gutierrez, Sally Bishop, Jo Mason and Dillon Morrall

Rhiannon Bevan-John and her colleagues at Christie's

Mitzi Mina and her colleagues at Sotheby's

Alison Mann and Pommery

Peretti Communications

Fiona Campbell, Amorim, Michael Cox and Rosamund Hitchcock

Wines of South Africa

Richard Caton of Bloomsbury Auctions

Beau Jarvis of Basicjuice.com

Nina Peek, Jessica Dorfman, Barbara Rosen, Helen Coates, Ellen Goldberg and Enrico Martinez, for the late nights and early mornings.

INTRODUCTION

There may have been times when more wine was drunk than it is now – a lot more. But it seems as if at no other time has wine been so much in the public consciousness.

Walk into nearly any decent-sized supermarket, and you'll be spoiled for choice – with row upon gleaming row of jewel-toned bottles, from two dozen countries or more. Visit any bookshop, and you'll find a multitude of guides to tasting wine; cooking with it; and travelling through the world's vineyards – not to mention tomes about wine's place in history and culture. Two wine-themed films – the controversial documentary *Mondovino* and the Hollywood confection *Sideways* – even made it onto cinema hit lists in 2004.

In the last few years, global wine production has been hovering at around 285 million hectolitres per year – over 38 billion bottles. That's roughly six bottles of wine for every person on the planet. But most of it is bland, boring, and just plain blah. It may be true that ultimately, we get the wine we deserve – that most people don't care what wine tastes like as long as it doesn't taste absolutely horrible, and the price is right.

But if you take a little time to learn about what you're drinking – about where it's made, and by whom – you'll find that almost everyone involved in the wine industry is there out of passion, not out of necessity. Sure, it's a business – and a competitive, difficult one, at that. But it's a business that people love, and with a little research and a splurge every now and again, you can find some of this love in a bottle.

Next time you have £20 burning a hole in your pocket, rather than buying four bottles for £5 each, ask an independent wine merchant what he or she would recommend if you were to plump for one bottle.

After all, life's too short to drink bad wine.

Maggie Rosen

WINE VOCABULARY 101

Learn these terms and you'll be able to bluff with the best of them...

Aroma: the part of a wine's smell that comes specifically from the grape variety (as opposed to other sources like the barrel, etc – see bouquet) – eg Sauvignon Blanc can smell grassy

Big: a powerful, strong wine – sometimes due to high alcohol content

Bouquet: the odour derived from the fermentation process; from the barrel; and from other conditional circumstances – independent of the grape variety. For example a Chardonnay with a buttery bouquet will have gone through a particular process called malolactic fermentation

Complex: multi-faceted, a wine that keeps you thinking

Late Harvest: when grapes are left past normal harvest time to ripen for longer; usually (but not always) this wine is sweeter and higher in alcohol

Residual sugar: the quantity of sugar that is left in a wine after the alcoholic fermentation is finished, and an indication of sweetness. The higher the quantity, the sweeter the wine

Tannin: a natural component of wine – reds in particular; a bitter-tasting element (also present in tea) which helps to preserve wine during ageing

WHEN AN ENTENTE PROVED CORDIALE

Britain had her first taste of French wine in the ninth century when a thin and rather tasteless wine was shipped from La Rochelle. But in the middle of the twelfth century, a great piece of good fortune fell our way. Henry II married Eleanor of Aquitaine and her dowry included all the west of France, including the great wine producing lands of the Médoc.

In a roundabout way, the popularity of wine from Médoc led to the creation of the modern British navy. Edward III issued currency regulations that forced the Bordeaux wine merchants to establish their bases on the French side of the Channel. Accordingly, the English had to build a fleet to fetch their wine.

IT'S THE WINE TALKING

There is a devil in every berry of the grape.
The Koran

GREAT WINE RECIPES

Coq au vin

It's not poulet au vin, you may note, it's coq – a dish designed to make the best of old strutting cocks once the lead's gone out of their pencils, not soft, damp, plumped up battery chickens. Find yourself a good older free-range bird from a proper butcher, weighing three and a half to four pounds. Something with a good gamey flavour to it.

Cut your chicken into six or eight pieces, taking the breasts off the carcass and dividing into two. Salt and pepper your chicken pieces. Chop the carcass into bits for swift stock-making, adding any oddments of bone or skin, a couple of onions and carrots cut up roughly and half a dozen peppercorns to a pan full of cold water. Bring to the boil, skim and set to simmer while you make everything else.

Cut five or six ounces of smoked bacon into lardons (small strips about half a centimetre thick – you need a piece of bacon to do this, not rashers). Put them in a casserole with a couple of lumps of butter and fry gently. Remove the bacon and fry your chicken pieces in the fat left behind until pale golden. Remove those too. Now fry off two large, roughly chopped onions and a big sliced carrot in the remaining fat, and don't worry if the pan's got a lot sticking to the bottom. Add two thinly sliced cloves of garlic and return the chicken and bacon to the pan.

Stir in two tablespoons of flour, cook for a couple of minutes then add a good slug of brandy and a bottle of red wine. Drop in a few bay leaves, a sprig of thyme and top up with your chicken stock until everything is covered. Bring to the boil, turn down to simmer and put the lid on. Cook for about 30 minutes, then melt two ounces of butter in a small pan and add 12 small onions – not shallots. Shake around then add half a pound of button mushrooms. When they're all golden slip the onions and mushrooms into the sauce to finish cooking – about another 20 minutes. If the sauce looks thin, leave the lid off to let it evaporate a bit.

IS THIS A DAGGER I SEE BEFORE ME?

The sight of someone beheading a bottle of Champagne is something to behold. Not merely the last word in stubborn cork removal, 'sabring' is a tradition that supposedly goes back to the Napoleonic era, when la Veuve Clicquot (the young widowed wife of the Champagne house owner) distributed bottles of Champagne to the soldiers she entertained. Unable to hold the reins of their rides and pop a cork at the same, the Hussards would draw their swords and lop the top off the bottle. Today, the Confrérie du Sabre d'Or, a society dedicated to the art of sabrage, upholds and promotes this tradition. Its 150-odd members – both male and female – fall into four ranks: Sabreur; Chevalier; Officier; and Commandeur –

depending on their skill level and length of membership. Members hold an official Diplôme de Sabrage, and meet in wine bars, hotels and other venues throughout the year, to practice. For sabreurs, only Champagne will do. Other sparkling wine bottles don't have the requisite seam and sweet spots that enable the sabreur to break the neck of the bottle in just the right place. According to the Confrérie, all you need is a firm wrist and a high elbow. 'When performed on a suitably chilled bottle of Champagne, the cork and glass annulus fly away, spilling little of the precious wine. The pressure of the Champagne always ensures that no glass falls back into the bottle.' Don't try this at home.

WORDS ON WINE

Many kinds of monkeys have a strong taste for tea, coffee, and spirituous liquors: they will also, as I have myself seen, smoke tobacco with pleasure... Brehm asserts that the natives of north-eastern Africa catch the wild baboons by exposing vessels with strong beer, by which they are made drunk. He has seen some of these animals, which he kept in confinement, in this state; and he gives a laughable account of their behaviour and strange grimaces. On the following morning they were very cross and dismal; they held their aching heads with both hands, and wore a most pitiable expression: when beer or wine was offered them, they turned away with disgust, but relished the juice of lemons... An American monkey, an Ateles, after getting drunk on brandy, would never touch it again, and thus was wiser than many men.

Charles Darwin, *Descent of Man* (1871)

WHAT IS THE DIFFERENCE BETWEEN ORGANIC AND BIODYNAMIC?

The essential difference between organic and biodynamic wine-making is that the rules of organic grape-growing tend to say 'don't do this or that' – it's a matter of leaving things out rather than adding them. Biodynamics, on the other hand, says 'do this or that' and is more about adding than subtracting. While some organic vineyards are therefore biodynamic, all biodynamic vineyards are organic. A great deal more work with compost preparations is involved with biodynamics than with organic methods, and it all has to be done in sync with the cycle of the moon.

Easy, really.

AREA UNDER VINE

Wine-growing countries in order of space allocated to grapevines

Spain	*1,200,000 hectares*
France	*900,000 hectares*
Italy	*884,000 hectares*
US	*411,000 hectares*
China	*390,000 hectares*
Portugal	*250,000 hectares*
Romania	*218,000 hectares*
Argentina	*210,000 hectares*
Chile	*183,000 hectares*
Australia	*157,500 hectares*
Greece	*123,000 hectares*
South Africa	*120,000 hectares*
Moldavia	*108,000 hectares*
Germany	*102,000 hectares*
Austria	*50,000 hectares*
New Zealand	*18,500 hectares*
UK + Luxembourg	*2,000 hectares*

*Figures are 2003 estimates, according to the
Organisation Internationale de la Vigne et du Vin*

BUT ISN'T ALL WINE VEGETARIAN?

Wine contains only grapes, yeast and a small amount of sulphites, but the processing of wine does introduce small amounts of clarifying agents not acceptable to many vegetarians and vegans. Some clarifiers are animal-based products, while others are earth-based. Here are the ones for vegetarians and vegans to avoid:

Egg whites: used for red wine clarification, especially expensive Burgundy wines or those French wines which are expected to age

Whole milk: possible fining agent for some red wines

Gelatine: used to clarify either red wine, white wine or beer and also used as a finishing agent to add the final touch to the quality and clarity of the wine without making any radical change in its flavour

Isinglass: prepared from the bladder of the sturgeon fish and used to fine selected white wines, especially in Germany. Some American fineries also use isinglass to clarify white wine

Blood: used in some Mediterranean countries but forbidden in France and the US

IT'S THE WINE TALKING

Wino Forever
Supposedly a tattoo on Johnny Depp's ankle. The tattoo originally read 'Winona Forever', but he had it altered after he and Ms Ryder split up.

JUST PLONK IT THERE

There are several explanations for the origin of 'plonk' – a derogatory term for cheap, inferior quality wine. Most evidence points to Australian soldiers in World War I, who, when encountering the French language for the first time, turned 'vin blanc' (white wine) into 'plonk.' There were many amusing variations including 'vin blank', 'von blink' and of course 'plinketty plonk'. After going through a phase where it came to mean moonshine, plonk was integrated into the regular lingo in the UK around the 1950s, when ordinary Brits began to drink French wine.

ALL GREEK TO ME

Today, many people find Greek wine less than agreeable because it is flavoured with resin or pine gum. This practice goes back to ancient times. After fermenting for nine to 10 days sweet hepsema (boiled down grape must) was added, and the wine poured into jars that had been smeared with pine cones as a preservative. Every five weeks, the jars were inspected and topped up with pine resin. As they are today, light wines were treated with resin as a preservative and in the spring the wine was bottled in amphorae.

This strong, resinous wine, like most Greek wine, was intended to be mixed with water. The Greeks regarded people who didn't mix their wine as barbarous. But there are also records of what appear to be Port-like wines being made by the Greeks, using grapes that had been left on the vine for a long time until syrupy and concentrated. Other experts have argued that this view of Greek wine may be due to confusion in translation of the words for 'sweet' and 'smooth' for 'rich' and 'easy to drink'.

WHEN IT'S OK TO BREAK A WINE GLASS...

A traditional Jewish wedding ceremony includes several rituals meant to signify the purpose of marriage in the context of history – several of these involve wine. Wine symbolises joy, and is associated with the Kiddush – a prayer of sanctification that is recited on the Sabbath (Saturday) and festival days. The marriage itself is called Kiddushin. Under a special canopy called a chupah, the engaged couple are presented with two cups of wine. After the Rabbi blesses the couple's betrothal, the couple drink from the first cup. Then the ring is given and the couple sign a marriage contract – called a ketubah. Next, the Rabbi says seven blessings over the second cup of wine, and the bride and groom then drink from this too. But as with many Jewish traditions, certain rites are meant to evoke history and remembrance as a caution for the future. A wine glass is placed on the floor and the groom smashes it with his heel. This signifies the violence and sadness associated with the destruction of the Temple in Jerusalem so that, even in life's happiest moments, Jews are reminded of the past and of their spiritual responsibilities for the future.

Of course the old Jewish joke is that this is the last time the groom gets to put his foot down. Mazel tov.

THROUGH A GLASS DARKLY

Which of the following is the name of a Spanish sparkling wine?

a) Prosecco

b) Fizziño

c) Cava

d) Frexa

Answer on page 153.

HOW TO IDENTIFY CRYSTAL GLASSES

Quite simply ping the rim and see if it sings... if you try it with a glass you know is crystal and one that isn't you'll soon learn the difference. Why do you need to know? Well for a start you need to keep crystal glasses out of dishwashers where the inner surface of the glass can get etched giving that ugly cloudy look. Once this has happened nothing can be done to revive the glass unless you want to have it professionally resurfaced (www.facetsglass.co.uk) for about £20 per item.

WHEN MARTINIS JUST AREN'T DE RIGUEUR

Bond's wines: Bollinger

In what may be his longest-lasting relationship, the cinematic James Bond (Sean Connery) has a thing for Bollinger in the 1971 film *Diamonds are Forever*. Roger Moore continues his penchant for Bolly in *Live and Let Die* (1973), ordering (but not always drinking) several bottles of undisclosed vintage. Likewise, in *Moonraker* (1979) Dr Holly Goodhead (Lois Chiles) offers Bond Bollinger '69. In *A View to a Kill* (1985) Roger Moore has a Bollinger '75 at the Jules Verne restaurant in the Eiffel Tower, and later orders a whole case of Bollinger R.D. (Recently Disgorged, a process whereby the wine is left to age on yeast lees for at least seven years). In *Licence to Kill* (1989), Timothy Dalton drinks no fewer than four glasses of Bollinger. In *GoldenEye* (1995) Pierce Brosnan has a bottle of the '88 vintage stashed away in his Aston Martin, while in *Die Another Day* (2002), he orders the '61 up to his Hong Kong hotel room. The vintage featured in *The World Is Not Enough* (1999) is reportedly the '90.

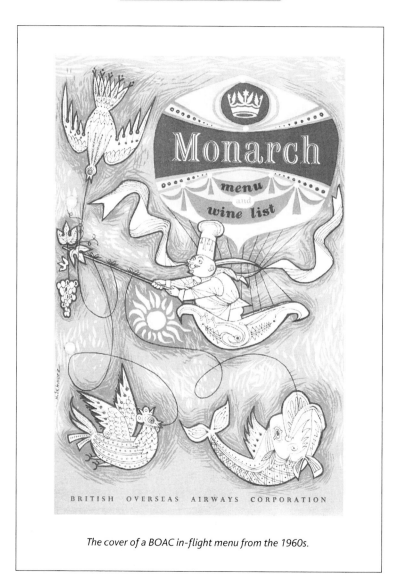

The cover of a BOAC in-flight menu from the 1960s.

ANY PORT IN A STORM?

Port has more mystique and ritual than any other wine. The tradition of passing the Port to the left may have come from the Navy – that is, that the Port was meant to be sent in the direction of port. According to tradition, the host tasted it first and then passed it with his left hand to the right hand of the person on his left, who served himself. The decanter would continue this way, clockwise around the table. The decanter should not cross the table or be touched by a lady (ladies were meant to drink Sherry). The left hand was meant to correspond with the heart, and allowed the right hand to remain free to reach for a sword in case of… emergency.

If for some reason the decanter didn't make its way back to the host, the host wasn't meant to ask for it directly, as that was considered impolite; rather, he was meant to ask the person closest to the decanter if he 'knows the bishop of Norwich or other village in England'. While the question was not meant to elicit an answer – but a quick reaction – if the person didn't take his cue, he would be told 'the bishop is an awfully good fellow, but he never passes the Port.'

Real Port lovers would never re-cork the bottle; rather, they would follow the 'no heel-tap' rule – the heel-tap being slang for the last drop in the bottle, from the peg in the heel of a shoe that a cobbler would remove when the shoe was finished. Drinking the Port to the last drop meant they could open another bottle.

ENOUGH TO SINK THE NAVY

Traditional Royal Navy toasts at sea:

Sunday	Absent Friends
Monday	Our Ships at Sea
Tuesday	Our Men
Wednesday	Ourselves
Thursday	Bloody War and a Sickly Season (for a more rapid promotion)
Friday	A Willing Foe and Plenty of Sea Room (in which to defeat them)
Saturday	Sweethearts and Wives (then, mumbled, 'may they never meet!')

WORDS ON WINE

A little maid of Astrakan,
An idol on a silk divan;
She sits so still, and never speaks,
She holds a cup of mine;
'Tis full of wine, and on her cheeks
Are stains and smears of wine.

Thou little girl of Astrakan,
I join thee on the silk divan:
There is no need to seek the land,
The rich bazaars where rubies shine;
For mines are in that little hand,
And on those little cheeks of thine.

**Richard Henry Stoddard,
'The Divan' from *Oriental Songs***

WINE WORDS

Ton

The word comes from a tun – a wine barrel. Tun comes from the French word 'tonnerre' – 'thunder' - from the sound the barrels made when rolled.

MONTY PYTHON AND THE HOLY MONTRACHET?

John Cleese, of *Monty Python* and *Fawlty Towers* fame, has recounted how Burgundy stopped him from committing suicide when he was severely depressed during the filming of *Monty Python and the Holy Grail*. Laid low by the appallingly dismal weather in Scotland, he drowned his sorrows in fine white wine at the bar of his hotel. 'It persuaded me to go on shooting the movie instead of shooting myself.'

GODS OF THE GRAPE

In the Egyptian pyramids you can find stand after stand of wine jars, each with their vintage, grape variety and vineyard clearly labelled. They wanted to have good wine to drink in the afterlife, and wine was particularly important as it was also an offering that could be made to almost all of the numerous gods and goddesses in the Egyptian pantheon. But the goddess with particular influence over grape-growing and wine-making was Renentet (sometimes known as Ernutet or Renen-utet), the goddess of harvest and growth. Many wineries had a small shrine to her beside the press itself (possibly because of the precarious nature of wine production in Egypt), and her sigil would often be carved on the spout through which the pressed grape juice flowed into the receiving tank for fermentation.

Osiris was also worshiped as a wine god, as was the Hathor, the goddess of intoxication through wine.

THE WINE DARK SEA

For centuries Homeric scholars tried to explain why Homer frequently refers to the sea as 'wine dark'. Many elegiac passages have been written by scholars describing how at a certain hour, from a certain viewpoint, a certain bit of sea around Greece does look the colour of wine, honestly.

'Wine dark sea' is one of those filler phrases common in oral poetry, which help the reciter remember the lines and are a kind of comforting presence to the listener. The dawn will always be 'rosy-fingered', the sea 'wine dark', Odysseus is always 'crafty', and all's well with the world. While most classicists were trying to make the earth fit this description, others were asking different questions like 'How did the Ancient Greeks perceive colour?'

They certainly used blues in their art, and indigo dye for dark blue clothing. But, the latest theory goes, they did not perceive changes in hue in the same places as we do, so they had no blue skies and blue seas. The same phrase is used to describe the dark colour of a wide variety of objects, including oxen, leading to conclusion that the Homeric sea was just the same as the seas we see... they just had a different way of naming it.

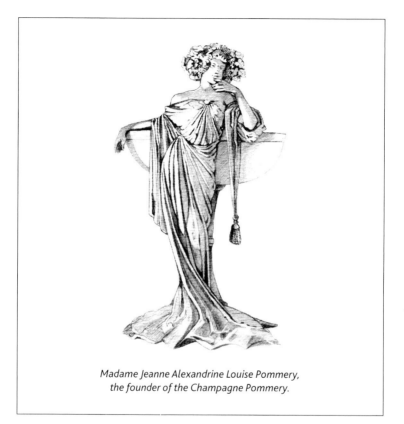

Madame Jeanne Alexandrine Louise Pommery,
the founder of the Champagne Pommery.

IT'S THE WINE TALKING

Thanks be to God, since my leaving drinking of wine, I do find myself much better, and do mind my business better, and do spend less money, and less time lost in idle company.
Samuel Pepys, from an entry in his Diary dated 26 January 1662

21

THROUGH A GLASS DARKLY

Try to unravel the following anagrams, all of which are varietals – from the everyday to the almost never.

a) BACON VANS LUG IN – hint: it's one of New Zealand's big hits

b)A LENTIL ROMP – hint: it's the main variety used in Rioja

c) LACING BUN – hint: rarely appears on its own, it's one of the main grapes used in Armagnac

d) VISAGE NOSE – hint: lots of this is drunk under the Tuscan sun

Answer on page 153.

USES FOR LEFTOVER WINE... AS IF!

- Freeze it in an ice tray and use the cubes in a fruit punch or sauces
- Use it in salad dressing instead of vinegar
- Put it in tomato or tomato-and-meat sauce
- Use it in a marinade for fish or meat
- Put it in a warm place with the right bacteria, it will be vinegar...

ROMAN WINE FLICKING

By way of entertainment after a meal, when strong wine was being drunk, young Romans might enjoy a few parlour games, including wine flicking or *Kottabus*. Each guest was given a shallow *krater* and had to flick wine from it at a mark on the floor.

Wine at banquets was served by slaves known as *Ministri* or *Pueri a Cyathothe*. They were chosen for their good looks and, whether male or female, usually had long curled hair and colourful clothing, and were regarded as the most important slaves within the serving hierarchy. A more raunchy version of *Kottabus* involved an attractive *Ministri* holding an empty vessel, into which each competitor in turn tried to flick wine. The one who succeeded in getting the most in the *Ministri's* vessel also got the *Ministri* for the night.

FOR MEDICINAL PURPOSES ONLY

For years people have associated the drinking of red wine and fortified wines with developing gout. But a new study shows that while many types of alcohol do have an effect on the development of gout wine itself doesn't.

Gout is a painful condition that affects the joints. It's really a kind of inflammatory arthritis caused by uric acid crystals being deposited on the joints. These crystals stimulate the body's own immune system and the joint becomes intensely inflamed. The disease was well known in Renaissance England, and particularly common during the Restoration and Regency periods when it became particularly associated with over-indulgence and drunkenness.

But an American study of 50,000 men over 12 years found that alcohol was linked to an increased risk of developing gout but that beer was far more likely to cause problems. In the last 30 years the number of cases of gout have risen dramatically, but the study concluded that this was down to a variety of factors, including doctors seeing more people and therefore diagnosing more cases, our less active lifestyle, eating more red meat and drinking more alcohol.

Alcohol has an effect because it competes with uric acid for removal via the kidneys. The kidneys have an increased work-load dealing with the lactic acid produced by alcohol and so more uric acid circulates through the body and gets deposited. Also, increased alcohol in the body is thought to stimulate the production of other chemicals that can be converted into uric acid.

Drinking two bottles of beer a day makes you almost 50% more likely to develop gout. A couple of gins increase your risk by 15%. But two glasses of wine make no difference. Salut!

HOW TO RECOGNISE VINOUS CARICATURES

The Champagne Socialist

Says all the right things, appears to care a great deal about the plight of the great unwashed. Yet, while the magnanimous ideologies may point in the right... or is it left... direction, they remain in the office after the workday is over, when the Champagne Socialist rides in a chauffeur-driven car to a celebrity-studded film premiere.

HOW TO DEFINE ORGANIC WINE

Like anything else, grapes can be grown to the strict standards necessary for organic certification, and an increasing number of people are taking an interest in organic wine. In addition, many organic growers try to produce their crops in a way which doesn't interfere with the food chain or leach contaminants into the water table. An organic wine will have been made with no trace of synthetic pesticide, fungicide or herbicide and no artificial fertilisers.

The grey areas are:

- The labels: wine is not subject to the labelling restrictions of all the other foodstuffs on sale in the UK.
- Even some organic farmers use copper sulphate and lime to combat mildew.
- Most have to resort to using minuscule amounts of sulphur as a preservative or the wine would be at risk of turning sour and brown within two months of bottling.

IT'S THE WINE TALKING

What contemptible scoundrel has stolen the cork from my lunch?
Larson E Whipsnade, played by WC Fields in *You Can't Cheat an Honest Man* (1939)

BUTT OF ALL THE JOKES

Richard III enjoys, with Henry VIII, the reputation of being one of the all-time baddies of British history, famously vilified by Shakespeare among many others. But it is hard to see how even he managed to have the Duke of Clarence drowned in a butt of malmsey, since the only opening would have been the bung through which the wine was drawn, and the casks were usually stored on their sides, not standing on end. The Duke would have thought it rum indeed to be invited to inspect a barrel of wine open at the top, although he has come down through history as a man with a fair thirst on him.

As an apocryphal story, it is a great one, but only one fact can be verified with certainty. The butt of Malmsey in which the dirty deed was done would have come from Cyprus.

WORDS ON WINE

For a good scare, read The Cask of Amontillado *(1846) by Edgar Allan Poe – Warning: this excerpt gives away the end!*

A succession of loud and shrill screams, bursting suddenly from the throat of the chained form, seemed to thrust me violently back. For a brief moment I hesitated -- I trembled. Unsheathing my rapier, I began to grope with it about the recess; but the thought of an instant reassured me. I placed my hand upon the solid fabric of the catacombs , and felt satisfied. I reapproached the wall. I replied to the yells of him who clamoured. I reechoed – I aided – I surpassed them in volume and in strength. I did this, and the clamourer grew still.

It was now midnight, and my task was drawing to a close. I had completed the eighth, the ninth, and the tenth tier. I had finished a portion of the last and the eleventh; there remained but a single stone to be fitted and plastered in. I struggled with its weight; I placed it partially in its destined position. But now there came from out the niche a low laugh that erected the hairs upon my head. It was succeeded by a sad voice, which I had difficulty in recognising as that of the noble Fortunato. The voice said –

'Ha! ha! ha! – he! he! – a very good joke indeed – an excellent jest. We will have many a rich laugh about it at the palazzo – he! he! he! – over our wine – he! he! he!'

'The Amontillado!' I said.

'He! he! he! – he! he! he! – yes, the Amontillado . But is it not getting late? Will not they be awaiting us at the palazzo, the Lady Fortunato and the rest? Let us be gone.'

'Yes,' I said 'let us be gone.'

'For the love of God, Montresor!'

'Yes,' I said, 'for the love of God!'

But to these words I hearkened in vain for a reply. I grew impatient. I called aloud –

'Fortunato!'

No answer. I called again –

'Fortunato!'

No answer still. I thrust a torch through the remaining aperture and let it fall within. There came forth in return only a jingling of the bells. My heart grew sick – on account of the dampness of the catacombs. I hastened to make an end of my labour. I forced the last stone into its position; I plastered it up. Against the new masonry I re-erected the old rampart of bones. For the half of a century no mortal has disturbed them.

In pace requiescat!

Edgar Allan Poe, *The Cask of Amontillado* (1846), *in which the main character, wine connoisseur Montresor, gets his revenge on Fortunato, an acquaintance who has been insulting him.*

SINGERS WITH WINE ON THEIR MIND

Days of Wine & Roses (Henry Mancini 1962,
sung by Johnny Mercer, Andy Williams and others)

Wine and Women (Bee Gees 1965)

Champagne Supernova (Oasis 1995)

Red, Red, Wine (Neil Diamond 1968, covered by UB40 and others)

Blood Red Wine (The Rolling Stones 1968)

Bottle of Red Wine (Eric Clapton 1970)

Bitter Wine (Jon Bon Jovi 1995)

Elderberry Wine (Elton John 1973)

Kisses Sweeter than Wine (The Weavers 1951)

Bottle of Wine (Tom Paxton 1965)

Cherry Red Wine (Jonny Lang 1998)

Dandelion Wine (The Hollies 1970)

WORDS ON WINE

O thou that high thy head dost bear
With round, smooth neck and simple ear,
With well-turn'd narrow mouth from whence
Flow streams of noblest eloquence
Tis thou that first'st the bard divine
Sacred to Phoebus and the nine;
That mirth and soft delight can move
Sacred to Venus and to Love
Yet, spite of all thy virtues rare
Thou'rt not a boon companion fair
Thou'rt full of wine when thirsty I,
And when I'm drunk then thou art dry

Alexander Webber, 'The Decanter'
from *Webber on Wine* (1888)

DRINKIN' WINE SPO-DEE-O-DEE
(OR SPODIODI... OR SPOODIE ODIE OR...)

However you spell it, 'Drinkin' Wine' is one of those songs, like 'Stagolee Shot Billy', that has been covered by dozens of artists, changed, rearranged, done up tempo and shot through with tragedy. Most people associate it with Jerry Lee Lewis, who played it as a rollicking piano boogie number with the opening shriek 'Down in New Orleans everything is fine/All them cats just drinkin that wine'.

Granville 'Stick' McGee, younger brother of the better known Brownie McGee, actually wrote the song during the war, except the chorus ran 'Drinking wine mother****er, drinkin wine'. He changed the lyrics to spo-dee-o-dee and had a hit with it in 1946 and then re-recorded it for Atlantic Records with a rocking beat in 1949, which in turn inspired the Jerry Lee version. A wine spodiodi is a wine cocktail made from port with a shot of bourbon poured carefully on top, followed by another measure of port.

IT'S THE WINE TALKING

If God forbade drinking, would He have made wine so good?
Armand Jean du Plessis, Cardinal and Duc de Richelieu

ALL GREEK TO ME

At an Athenian banquet, the Greeks ate lightly and only started to drink when the meal was finished. Serving girls were sent to the nearest well house to fetch cold spring water to be mixed with the wine, which was brought up from the cellar in storage amphorae and decanted into smaller and more elegant amphorae. Occasionally, it was poured into vases, often painted, which were packed with ice. Oddly, there were pictures on the wine vessels but no frescos on the walls, and painted vessels became the focus of Greek decorative art for many decades.

Greek vases were certainly works of art, but they were not on a par with those of the Egyptians, who used not only clay, but hard stone, alabaster, glass, ivory, bone, porcelain, bronze, silver and gold for their wine vessels.

IF AT FIRST YOU DON'T SUCCEED... GIVE UP

One summer day, a Fox was strolling through an orchard and came upon a bunch of grapes just ripening on a vine which had been trained over a lofty branch. 'Just the things to quench my thirst,' he said. Drawing back a few paces, he took a run and a jump, and just missed the bunch. Turning round again, he counted one, two, three, and jumped up again – but with no greater success. Again and again he tried to reach the grapes but at last had to give it up, and walked away with his nose in the air, saying: 'I am sure they are sour'.

The Fox and the Grapes, a fable by Aesop (sixth century BC)

TOP BORDEAUX VINTAGES FROM OVER 200 YEARS OF CLARET-MAKING

2000	1982	1961
1953	1947	1945
1929	1900	1899
1874	1870	1864
1847	1811	1798

WINE WORDS

Honeymoon

There are several explanations for the origin of this word. In ancient Babylon, a bride's father would supply his son-in-law with all the mead (fermented honey beverage) he could drink for a month after the wedding. Weddings commonly took place during the Summer solstice, when honey was being harvested. The drink supposedly increased virility and fertility. And because the calendar used at the time was lunar, this period of free mead was called the 'honey month', or what we now call the 'honeymoon'. One of the first references in the Oxford English Dictionary indicates that although honeymoon today has a positive meaning, it was actually a sarcastic reference to love waning like a phase of the moon. Of course a bit of Champagne – or indeed mead – can help restore a couple to their original state of bliss. But too much will have the opposite effect.

ODE TO A NIGHTINGALE

In John Keats's famous poem about longing and ennui the drinking motif runs throughout, from the first lines describing a lassitude 'as though of hemlock I had drunk'. In the second verse the weary narrator wants 'a draught of vintage! that hath been/Cool'd a long age in the deep-delved earth/Tasting of Flora and the country green/Dance, and Provençal song, and sunburnt mirth!' harking back to his travels in southern Europe and the custom of burying things to keep them cool in the hot climate. He goes on to ask for 'a beaker full of the warm South, full of the true, the blushful Hippocrene,' referring to wine made with water from the spring supposedly created by Pegasus the winged horse's hooves on the side of Mt Helicon. Mt Helicon is, of course, the home of the muses in classical mythology, and the Hippocrene spring is said to be the fountain of poetic inspiration.

WORDS ON WINE

It occurs to me to discuss wine and hashish in the same article, because they have something in common: both cause a significant poetic evolution in men. Man's greatness is attested by his craving for all things – healthy or otherwise – that encourage his individuality. He seeks always to rekindle his hopes and rise to infinity. But we must examine the results. On one hand, we have a beverage that helps digestion, strengthens the muscles, and enriches the blood. Even when taken in large quantities, it causes only relatively short-lived disorders. On the other hand, we have a substance that impedes the digestive processes, weakens the limbs and is capable of producing an intoxication that lasts up to 24 hours. Wine exalts the will, hashish destroys it. Wine is a physical support, hashish a self-destructive weapon. Wine makes a man good-natured and sociable, hashish isolates him. The one is industrious, as it were; the other, essentially lazy. Indeed, what point is there in working, toiling, writing, creating anything at all when it is possible to obtain Paradise in a single swallow? In a word, wine is for the working man, who deserves to drink of it. Hashish belongs to the class of solitary pleasures; it is made for the pitiful creatures with time on their hands. Wine is useful, it yields fruitful results. Hashish is useless and dangerous.

Charles-Pierre Baudelaire, *On Wine and Hashish* (1851)

IT'S THE WINE TALKING

I rather like bad wine… one gets so bored with good wine.
Benjamin Disraeli, Earl of Beaconsfield and Prime Minister

GLOBAL WARMING AND WINE

While wine connoisseurs scan harvest records in pursuit of the perfect vintage, oenologists (winemakers) are agonising over whether those same records will reveal any insights into whether harvest dates and conditions have changed in response to the phenomenon of global warming. For every year in the last decade or so, it seems one of the major wine regions of the world experiences extreme conditions of some kind (drought, rain, frost).

Or perhaps it's just that we're starting to notice and talk about it. One US phenology study (relationship between growth and climatic conditions) analysed 50 years of climate data across over 25 regions, comparing the results with the 100-point vintage ratings of Sotheby's auction house, to determine whether there was any correlation between quality and growing-season temperatures. This study showed that growth-season temperatures have increased by 2°C over the last 50 years in most regions known for producing high quality wine, and that the quality of vintages has also improved – indicating a positive correspondence between temperature and

quality. Yet, during that same period, both vinification and agricultural techniques have improved. Likewise, there is some indication that climate in general has fluctuated over this period of time.

Last but not least, while regions like Bordeaux and Burgundy – which have been keeping records for many centuries – have experienced record-breaking high temperatures and other extremes in recent years, over long periods of time there is little to no change in the start-date and length of the harvest season, indicating that what we're seeing now is a brief – albeit dramatic – phase. While such a short-term warming trend may be good for producers on the winemaking fringe – those in England, for example – hotter seasons and earlier harvest start dates may be problematic for regions that are already warm: too much heat can lead to over-ripening and higher-than-acceptable alcohol levels; water shortages; pests; and other heat-related issues. Like the debates over climate change and other aspects of agricultural and industrial development, discussions about the hows, whys and whethers of the weather are sure to run and run.

GREAT WINE RECIPES

Wine jelly

In adulthood we tend to forget the shivery, sugary delight of jelly. By throwing out the packets and getting acquainted with the use of leaf gelatine you can make deliciously boozy jellies using all sorts of wine. As a rough guide one sheet of gelatine will set 100ml of alcoholic liquid, so for a litre you would need 10 sheets. Wine on its own, unless it's sweet, tends to be a bit sour for jelly, so you can mix it with fruit juice, or use Port or other fortified wine to balance the sweetness, using about half a pint to a pint of wine. That said, a fruity and zingy wine like an Australian Riesling can make an interesting jelly when paired with a very smooth, sweet fruit like mango.

To make a fruit jelly put your gelatine sheets in a little cold water to soften them. Meanwhile, warm your wine mixture. Squeeze out the sheets, drop into the warm (but not hot) liquid, and stir until dissolved, then pour into a mould and leave to set somewhere cold.

If the idea of serving a big quivery lump doesn't appeal, take the set jelly and slice it into little pieces. You can do a couple of colours and mix them. They look quite magical by candle-light, sparkling, served with fruit.

A MATTER OF TASTE

Have you ever stopped to think about the 'tastes' your tongue can perceive? Most people are familiar with the first four, the last one has come to our attention relatively recently...

Sweet: can feel a bit tingly – too much can feel like it's coating your mouth

Sour: a mouth-puckering sensation, can make your eyes water

Bitter: imparts a somewhat drying sensation, makes you want to run your tongue against the top of your mouth

Salty: gives you a thirsty feeling but even some wines are described as being slightly salty

Umami: the new 'mystery guest', a pungent, smoky-sweet taste that makes you want to eat more; you know it when you taste it...

THROUGH A GLASS DARKLY

While taking a romantic balloon ride off the coast of Spain, a honeymooning couple dropped two 750ml bottles of Cava (Spanish sparkling wine) over the side. If one bottle had been drunk, and the other was still full, which hit the ground first? *Answer on page 153.*

WHAT AM I BID?

Auctions are a great place to pick up a wine bargain or an oddity, and anyone can participate. The big names in UK wine auctions are Christie's and Sotheby's, followed by Bonhams and Straker Chadwick. But before you raise your paddle, you really need to do your homework. Read the catalogues scrupulously but know they're written by human beings, and not always infallible ones. Check the market prices of anything you plan to bid on, and go to pre-sale tastings if possible. Caveat bidder – auctioneers will only take something back under exceptional circumstances.

The most expensive bottle of wine ever sold at auction: Château Lafite 1787, marked Th.J. (i.e. Thomas Jefferson, US President) sold for £105,000 in 1985 at Christie's in London.

Most expensive white wine ever sold: also associated with Thomas Jefferson – 1787 Château d'Yquem, for $56,588 (though not quite an urban myth, nobody seems to recall where or when it was sold).

Most expensive bottle of wine that's still drinkable today (and the most expensive ever sold in the US): 1978 Domaine de la Romanée-Conti sold by Sotheby's for $23,929 per bottle (as part of a seven bottle lot sold totalling $167,500).

Most expensive (standard-sized) bottle of Port ever sold at auction: Quinta do Noval Nacional 1931, in 1988 by Christie's, for $1,100. A bottle of this same Port also sold for $5,900 at the Graycliff Restaurant in the Bahamas.

The largest bottle of Port ever sold: a 30-litre bottle (holding 40 single bottles) of Taylor's 1963, by Sotheby's in 1999, sold for $19,550. This broke the Christie's record for the same size bottle of the same Port sold in 1995 for £9,900 ($15,000).

The world's largest bottle of wine: holding the equivalent of 173 regular bottles

(1,200 glasses) of 2001 Beringer Private Reserve Cabernet Sauvignon, sold for $47,000 at Sotheby's in 2004. A Bordeaux-style bottle dubbed Maximus, it was specially-commissioned by Morton's Steakhouse, and measured 4ft 5in tall, by 4ft 5in around. Proceeds went to charity.

Most expensive bottle of wine ever… broken: a bottle of Château Margaux 1787, brought to a Châteaux Margaux dinner at the Four Seasons restaurant… broken by a waiter carrying a coffee tray. Luckily it was insured for $500,000, far more than the value of the wine. The same may not be said of the waiter…

Most expensive corkscrew ever sold: an English early/mid eighteenth-century silver pocket corkscrew, engraved on the handle E.H., 1 November 1743, additionally engraved with A.R. Alexandra Regina, from the Queen, 1910 (the wife of Edward VII) sold by Christie's for £18,400 in 1997.

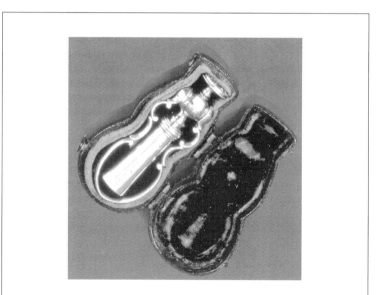

From the Doctor Bernard Whatney Collection: the corkscrew that drew the highest price ever paid for a corkscrew.

TO YOU, AND YOU, AND YOU

*There are as many ways to say 'cheers' as there are
countries that make wine – and then some.*

Afrikaans: *Gesondheid*

Arabic: *Shucram*

Cantonese: *Yung sing!* (something like 'Drink and win')

Danish: *Skaal/Skål*

Danish – alternative: *Bunden i vejret eller resten i håret*
(Bottoms up or the rest in your hair!)

Fijian: *Ni bula*

Finnish: *Kippis* or *Maljanne*

French: *À votre santé* (To your health) –
response is *À la votre* (And to yours)

German: *Prost*

Hebrew: *L'chaim* (To life)

Irish (Gaelic): *Sláinte*

Japanese: *Kampai*

Korean: *Combay*

Italian: *Salute*, or *Cin cin* (Chin chin)

Maori: *Kia ora* (Be of good health)

Portuguese: *Saude* (To your health)

Russian: *Na zdorovje* (To your health)

Samoan: *Ta manuia* (Happiness)

Spanish: *Salud* (Catalan: *Salut*)

Ukrainian: *Budmo* (May we live forever)

ALL GREEK TO ME

The Ancient Greeks divided wine into three sorts: red, amber and straw-coloured. The Romans went one better. They enjoyed black wines, blood wines, amber and straw-coloured, dividing what we'd recognise as reds into two different categories.

USA 2, FRANCE 0

Until about three quarters of the way through the twentieth century, France dominated the world's wine industry, if not quite in quantity, then in quality. In good years and bad, through high times and low, the reputation of France's best wines is such that it had always found high praise and willing buyers. But something happened in 1976 from which the French have never fully recovered. A young wine merchant named Steven Spurrier (now a world-renowned authority) staged a wine tasting in Paris, pitting French wines against Californian wines of the same vintages. It was to be a 'blind' tasting, so participants were not told what they were trying.

Assuming the French would win hands-down, Spurrier thought the tasting would attract some attention and confirm France's position as quality leader. He invited French wine experts and food writers, and set up a blind tasting of chardonnays (French Burgundy vs Californians). The results shocked everyone: the winner was the Napa Valley 1973 Château Montelena – beating the 1973 Meursault-Charmes Burgundy. Californians also won third and fourth place. Yet the French tasters made such remarks as: 'This one is definitely from California

– it has no nose' (of the 1973 Batard Montrachet from Burgundy).

Next up came the reds, and since reds are considered more prestigious, Spurrier decided to let the tasters know the results of the whites test – at which point they became even more resolved to pick a French red as the winner. So confident in their ability to spot French characteristics of quality, they denigrated what they were sure were American wines. Once again, the winner was an American wine – 1973 Stag's Leap Wine Cellars Cabernet Sauvignon (Napa Valley). The French press attempted to downplay the results, but George Taber, a young American journalist from Time magazine wrote a little story that took on a life of its own. The results made headlines, and the wine world woke up. Two years later, the Smithsonian Institute in Washington DC added a bottle each of the winning white and red wines to their collection to highlight the importance to American history of the 1976 Paris tasting.

These days, wine drinkers know that great wine can be made nearly anywhere as long as the conditions are right. Today, the French are still convinced they were tricked – and Taber has written a book (*The Judgment of Paris*) to set the record straight.

WINE TRENDS THAT BECAME CORKED

White wine spritzers	So 1970s and such a waste of wine, good or bad
Blue Nun	Another 1970s phenomenon, this time from Germany; so pernicious has its reputation been that good German wine remains a bargain to this day
Wine coolers	Went out with the last century, and good riddance. If you want fruit in your wine, have a sangria!
Beaujolais Nouveau	A great marketing ploy to get us to drink early and often a mostly low-quality wine; it's being phased out as Beaujolais grows up
Over-oaked Chardonnay	We like our butter-slathered toast for breakfast, thank you very much!

FOR MEDICINAL PURPOSES ONLY

Wine played an important part in Greek medicine. Hippocrates, whose approach would be followed until the sixteenth century, believed that the body contained four humours or liquids (black bile, blood, yellow bile and phlegm), which corresponded to the four elements. Having too much or too little of these humours caused imbalance and therefore disease. 'Black bile like wine is prone to ferment and produce an alternation of depression and anger,' said Aristotle.

A Greek physician's first step would be to observe the patient and then prescribe a new diet and exercise regimen to try and redress the balance. If the patient was feverish, caused by yellow bile which was associated with hot and dry things, then they would be given a series of cold baths. If they had a cold, and were producing a lot of phlegm, then they were wrapped up cozily and told to drink warming wine.

If this didn't help – and you can imagine that in many cases it would – then the physician would resort to drugs, often hellebore, a poison that provoked vomiting and diarrhoea. This 'productive' method was seen as a sign that the body had got rid of the excess humour, and was therefore cured. The limited amount of prescriptions probably meant that most Greeks survived a visit from the doctor, and indeed felt better afterwards. In later centuries the doctor often proved to be deadlier than the disease he was called in to treat.

CHAMPAGNE CHARLIES

If the aunt of the vicar has never touched liquor,
watch out when she finds the Champagne.
Rudyard Kipling

Remember gentlemen, it's not just France we are fighting for, it's Champagne!
Winston Churchill

Here's Champagne to your real friends and real pain to your sham friends.
Anon

Here's to Champagne, the drink divine,
That makes us forget all our troubles;
It's made of a dollar's worth of wine
And three dollars' worth of bubbles.
Anon

I was too exhausted even to eat until I had drunk half a bottle of Champagne,
after which I slept like a log.'
Aleister Crowley, upon climbing 5,000 feet into the Himalayas

Champagne has the taste of an apple peeled with a steel knife.
Aldous Huxley

HOW TO RECOGNISE VINOUS CARICATURES

The Flying Winemaker

A recent phenomenon, this evolving species of oenologists work as paid consultants to multiple wineries around the world. They literally fly from client to client, check on conditions in the vineyard, winery and cellar, and impart advice to the local winemaker-in-charge. While the benefits to the winery are many – not least, being associated with a famous name can make a reputation – critics of the phenomenon say that wines under a flying winemaker's care run the risk of losing their uniqueness.

WORDS ON WINE

Before I get to a more positive approach, let me describe, in careful stages, not what you should do when serving wine to your guests, but what you nearly always do (if you are anything like me):

1. Realise that They will be arriving in less than an hour and you have done damn-all about it.

2. Realise, on your way to the cellar or wherever you keep the stuff, that the red wine to go with the roast beef will be nowhere near the required room temperature if left to warm up unassisted.

3. Realise, on reaching the stuff, that it has not had time to 'settle' after being delivered, and that you should have realised six weeks – or, if you had wanted to give Them a treat, 10 years – ago exactly what wine you were going to need tonight.

4. Decide that They can bloody well take what They are given, grab some bottles and take them to the kitchen.

5. Take the foil off the necks of the bottles (now that the bottlers have mostly decided they can cut costs by leaving the lead out of this, your present task is like removing nail-polish with a fish-knife).

6. Look for the corkscrew.

7. Having (we will assume) found the corkscrew, unscrew the cork that somebody has left screwed on it and open the bottles.

8. Find something to take the gunk or crap off the bottlenecks and take it off.

9. Decide that, while any fool can tell when wine is cold, and nearly any fool knows nowadays that a red wine is not supposed to be cold, hardly anyone knows a decent glass of it from a bad one, and stick the bottles in a saucepan of warm water.

10. Spend parts of the next hour-and-a-half wondering whether old Shagbag, who is reputed to know one wine from another, will denounce you for boiling out whatever quality tonight's stuff might have had, or will suffer in the silence. Also wonder whether the others will think 1971 a rather insultingly recent year for a Médoc, whether to get up another bottle on the off-chance that They can force down what you have 'prepared' for the table, whether to oil that too or bank on Their being too drunk to notice or too polite to mention its coldness, and kindred questions.

11. Do not enjoy the wine much yourself when you come to drink it.

Kingsley Amis, 'First Thoughts on Wine' from *On Drinking* (1972)

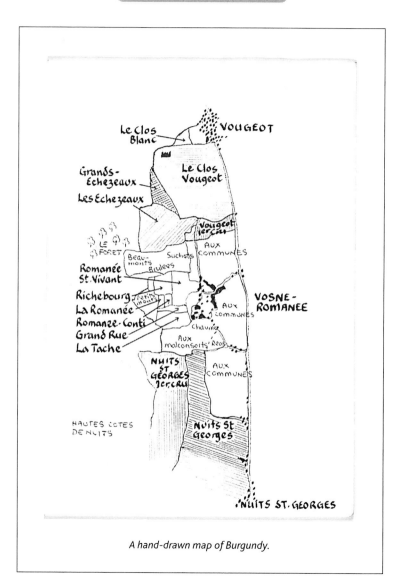

A hand-drawn map of Burgundy.

YOU KNOW YOU'RE A WINE GEEK WHEN...

- You'd sooner spend that last £50 on one bottle of £50 wine, than on 10 bottles of £5 wine
- You keep labels
- You carry a vintage chart in your wallet instead of photos of your children
- You know more about wine than current world conflicts
- You buy a wine fridge that costs as much as a luxury holiday
- You have more wine than books
- You name your pets or children after wines
- You find yourself swirling and sniffing your water glass
- In a restaurant, you take longer to order wine than food
- Wine is what you'd choose to save when running from a burning building
- You spend more time thinking about wine than about sex
- Your wine is worth more than your pension
- You think raisins are a waste of a good grape
- When someone says 'red, white and...' you think 'rosé'
- You own more wine glasses than cutlery

IT'S THE WINE TALKING

The last time that I trusted a dame was in Paris in 1940. She was going out to get a bottle of wine. Two hours later, the Germans marched into France.
Sam Diamond, played by Peter Falk, in *Murder by Death* (1976)

WHEN BRIDES ATTACK

Someone should have told German-born Amy Weltz that it's an old Australian tradition for the bride and groom to smear wedding cake on each other's faces after cutting it. At their reception in Brisbane, in 1993, her new husband Chas duly reached for a slice and rubbed it into her face. The shocked and outraged Amy grabbed a wine bottle from the table and hit him over the head, killing him instantly.

THROUGH A GLASS DARKLY

You may know the three main grape varieties that go into Champagne – but did you know there are actually six permitted varieties? See if you can name them – and bonus points for guessing which are red and which are white.
Answer on page 153.

FOR ALL THE WINE IN CHINA

Believe it or not, the wine industry in China is booming – so much so that it's starting to attract the attention of foreign beverage conglomerates like Castel Frères (owners of Nicolas and Oddbins wine chains, among other things) and Les Grands Chais de France. Salivating at the prospect of a combination of great tracts of land; cheap labour; and a potentially huge market for their products, French, American and Australian wine producers have forged joint ventures with Chinese producers. For although China's per capita wine consumption is just half a litre – trailing well behind the average global per capita consumption of 7.5 litres – from 1994 to 2000, consumption grew by a whopping 61.8%, and leading domestic producer Changyu has estimated that demand will continue to grow by 8–10% per year. With one fifth of the world's population, that's a lot of wine. China claims to have over around 180,000 acres of vineyard – much of it in remote areas. But increasingly, producers have their sights set on Shandong Province, which supposedly lies more or less along the same parallel as Napa Valley. Most domestic wine is made from indigenous grapes blended with low quality imported bulk wine. But with an increase in domestic grape cultivation and better production techniques, imports are dropping.

Yet China has long had a history of wine production, and boasts at least one 'wine town'. Turpan (aka Turfan), which has been described as a wine theme park, is located in the Turpan depression (Xinjiang Uygur Autonomous Region) of northwestern China, the second lowest point in the world after the Dead Sea. From 200–400AD, the region was the centre of a flourishing Indian and Persian civilisation that was later integrated into that of the Uygurs. Turpan has reinvented itself as a tourist destination and agricultural oasis, famous for its grapes; nearly everyone in the town is involved in grape cultivation. Just east of Turpan is the so-called Grape Valley, filled with trellised walkways that are covered with bunches of grapes during peak season.

41

WHEN MARTINIS JUST AREN'T DE RIGUEUR

Bond's wines: Dom Pérignon

Can you say product placement? Bond knows his champers, and this time it's Dom
Pérignon. In *Dr. No* (1962) Sean Connery tries to knock his nemesis out with a bot-
tle of DP '55 (remarking 'I prefer the '53 myself'). He also prefers the '53 in
Goldfinger (1964), but in *Thunderball* (1965) he deviates and orders a bottle of '55
– and in *You Only Live Twice* (1967) he drinks a '59. In *On Her Majesty's Secret
Service* (1969) George Lazenby plumps for '57, while in *The Man with the Golden
Gun* (1974), when offered the '64, Moore comments 'I prefer the '62 myself.'
Finally, in *The Spy Who Loved Me* (1977), he makes his famous declaration about
Stromberg, that 'Any man who drinks Dom Pérignon '52 can't be all bad.'

HOW TO SEND WINE BACK POLITELY

We don't like to do it, but every wine drinker will, one day, be faced with the task of
sending a bottle of wine back in a restaurant. Customers are perhaps becoming more
aware of suspect wine, with various sources suggesting that between one in 10 and
one in five bottles are reported as faulty to some degree.

First of all, bear in mind that you are the customer, you are the person paying for the
wine. If the wine tastes bad to you, you have every right to send it back. Have the
courage of your convictions. Often people hesitate to send back slightly corked wine
because they don't trust their own senses.

Try to make as little fuss as possible. Don't call the waiter over and loudly announce
to the whole room that the wine tastes funny. But be firm and unapologetic. Say 'This
wine is off, please bring me another bottle.' Don't say 'Er, I'm afraid I think there's
something wrong with the wine...' Give an instruction, don't leave them to decide on
the appropriate action. A good waiter will calmly whisk away the offending bottle and
replace it with another of the same wine. If he tries to give you a different wine
(some waiters will try and suggest you don't have the taste to understand the
complex flavours of the wine you've just returned, rather than accepting that it
smells like a mix of musty newspapers and damp dog), explain in simple language
that corking is something that only happens occasionally and it's not the whole batch
of wine that tastes amiss.

TEN THINGS YOU MIGHT NOT KNOW ABOUT AUSTRALIAN WINE

1. Although it is a huge country, the whole of Australia makes less wine than the Bordeaux region in France

2. On average, a new winery opens in Australia every day – 377 opened in 2004

3. The most widely planted white grape is Chardonnay

4. The most widely planted red grape is Shiraz

5. Wine is made near Alice Springs in Australia's red-hot red centre

6. Victoria has the most wineries of any state in Australia

7. The oldest Shiraz vines in the world (born in 1860) are at the Tahbilk estate in Victoria

8. Although you will often find 'South East Australia' on labels, there is no such state

9. Jacob's Creek is a real place, just up the road from Orlando Wyndham's winery

10. Winemaking in Margaret River was largely established by doctors – proof that wine is good for you

IT'S THE WINE TALKING

Ah, make the most of what we yet may spend,
Before we too into the Dust descend;
Dust into Dust, and under Dust, to lie,
Sans Wine, sans Song, sans Singer, and – sans End!
From *The Rubáiyát of Omar Khayyám*, translated by Edward FitzGerald (1859)

ELIZABETH THE GREAT

Good Queen Bess might have been desperately in need of money at her accession to the English throne in 1558 but she felt that it was wrong to tax her subjects unduly on wine. Through most of her reign the wine tax remained at a low level, and even this was only necessary because the King of France insisted that the wines of Bordeaux be transported in French 'bottoms' or vessels which had to be paid for.

WHO NEEDS BEER?

Wine consumption per person per year

1.	Italy	54 litres
2.	France	47 litres
3.	Switzerland	42 litres
4.	Austria	36 litres
5.	Denmark	32 litres
6.	Belgium	30 litres
7.	Germany	26 litres
8.	Australia	21 litres
9.	Netherlands	20 litres
10.	UK	20 litres
11.	New Zealand	19 litres
12.	Sweden	16 litres
13.	Ireland	13 litres
14.	Norway	11 litres
15.	Finland	10 litres
16.	Canada	10 litres
17.	Japan	10 litres
18.	United States	7 litres

Source: Euromonitor 2002

DON'T MYTH THIS

The race to be the most prestigious single vineyard wine is fierce, and nowhere more so than in Alsace, where the vineyard of Brand in Turckheim is assisted by a local legend. It was here in the Middle Ages that a battle took place between the sun and a local dragon. True to form, the dragon was engulfed in burning flames until nothing was left but a brand in the earth.

As a result, the soil was infused with a heat so fierce that the grapes would, for all eternity, have a dragon-like fiery quality of ripeness – and so it has proved with the elusive mixture of Pinot Noir grapes in Alsatian soil. But the Tokay-Pinot Gris is one of the finest wines produced by Brand today.

A-BANTING WE WILL GO

Centuries before anyone had thought of the Atkins diet a London carpenter of some considerable girth, one William Banting, devised and popularised his own version of the high protein, low carb regime. The only difference was Banting's diet allowed the dieter a considerable amount of alcohol to soften the hunger pangs – two or three glasses of claret, Port or Sherry with lunch, and the same with dinner. Of course, if you were accustomed to drinking a couple of bottles of these beverages with each meal it would seem like you were cutting down, but despite drinking sweet wine every day Banting still succeeded in losing about 50 pounds in as many weeks, reducing from 202lb to 156lb in a year.

In 1863 he wrote a book (*A Letter on Corpulance Addressed to the Public*) setting out his method, and it was so successful that 'to bant' became a common verb at the time, meaning to go on a diet.

WORDS ON WINE

ALGERNON: Oh! . . . by the way, Lane, I see from your book that on Thursday night, when Lord Shoreman and Mr. Worthing were dining with me, eight bottles of Champagne are entered as having been consumed.

LANE: Yes, sir; eight bottles and a pint.

ALGERNON: Why is it that at a bachelor's establishment the servants invariably drink the Champagne? I ask merely for information.

LANE: I attribute it to the superior quality of the wine, sir. I have often observed that in married households the Champagne is rarely of a first-rate brand.

ALGERNON: Good heavens! Is marriage so demoralising as that?

LANE: I believe it is a very pleasant state, sir. I have had very little experience of it myself up to the present. I have only been married once. That was in consequence of a misunderstanding between myself and a young person.

ALGERNON: I don't know that I am much interested in your family life, Lane.

LANE: No, sir; it is not a very interesting subject. I never think of it myself.

ALGERNON: Very natural, I am sure. That will do, Lane, thank you.

Oscar Wilde, *The Importance of Being Earnest* (1895)

THOU SHALT NOT DRINK... OFFICIALLY

Midnight on 16 January 1920 may have been a record-breaker for last orders in bars across the United States – for on 17 January, a 13-year Constitutionally-mandated dry spell known as Prohibition set in. Unsurprisingly, Prohibition ushered in an era of smuggling, bootlegging, and worse. For while commercial wine production and consumption in public places was banned, households were allowed to make 200 gallons of alcohol a year for their own consumption – a whopping three bottles a day, and criminal opportunists stepped in to control the sales and distribution channels.

The most famous of the gangsters was Al Capone, whose bootlegging ring was reported to have netted over $50m a year. Speakeasies – illegal drinking dens – sprang up everywhere, and ranged from seedy holes to fashionable secret clubs frequented by celebrities and politicians. Americans are nothing if not entrepreneurial, and one supposedly best-selling item invented during Prohibition was something called a grape brick, a compressed chunk of dried grape concentrate – purportedly for making grape juice – that came with a packet of yeast and strict instructions that said something to the effect of 'To make a refreshing grape-juice drink, dissolve contents in large pitcher of water', and on the reverse 'Caution: Never mix contents in two gallons of warm water to which you have added a pinch of yeast, and one pound of sugar. If this mixture is left to stand in a cloth covered container for two weeks, an illegal alcoholic beverage will result'.

No wonder then that, during Prohibition, consumption doubled that of pre-1920 levels. With so much crime and flagrant flouting of the law, it was finally repealed on 5 December 1933. The deciding vote in favour of repeal came from the State of Utah, which is somewhat ironic, as today Utah is possibly the most stringent regulator of alcohol in America. And although Prohibition only lasted 13 years, 10 months, 19 days, 17 hours and 32 minutes (according to wine educator Fred McMillin) – many would argue that the country itself is still in recovery. Seventy-two years after Prohibition was repealed, there are still many counties in the United States that do not allow the sale of alcoholic beverages (as an aside, in the State of Kentucky, Christian County is 'wet', while Bourbon County is 'dry'). Many others do not allow the sale of alcohol on Election Day; Sundays; Thanksgiving or Christmas. Likewise, tenacious and widespread negative attitudes toward alcohol, and an uneasy debate over whether alcohol is a drug and should be regulated persist.

IT'S THE WINE TALKING

Sparkling Moscatel. One of the finest wines of Idaho.
Steve Martin, as a waiter in *The Muppet Movie* (1979)

The Roman wine-god Bacchus as a baby.

PORT SNORT

During the yuppie 1980s the obscure art of Port snorting became suddenly fashionable. Although some claimed it was a historical activity being revived this seems to be a red herring. A capful of aged Port is held under one nostril, the other squeezed firmly shut and with a big 'huff' inhaled, the idea being that the alcohol is absorbed faster through the mucus membranes of the nose than when mixed with the contents of the stomach. In the 1990s young women began using the same principal to get drunk quickly by soaking tampons in spirits.

THROUGH A GLASS DARKLY

The clever Sommelier (wine server) fills one 5oz wine glass half full of white wine, and a 10oz glass one-third full of red wine. He then tops up each glass with water and pours the contents of both into a bucket. How much of the mixture in the bucket is wine and how much is water?

Answer on page 153.

SIPPS OF WINE FOR ALL...

From April 2006, UK wine lovers will be able to lay away a little something for a rainy day – and it can be red, white or rosé. As part of a dramatic pension reform initiative, wine will be one of the many assets that can be incorporated into both large-scale pension funds and SIPPS (self-invested personal pensions). This will mean that Premier Crus and vintage Champagnes could double as both tax relief and a fabulous retirement party. The fine wine insiders believe this will fundamentally change the market. Wine consultants may take on a new role as finan-cial advisors, since pension funds will require approvals from their trustees or managers before buying up those bottles. Likewise, if funds start taking large positions in wine, the market may become less liquid – pushing up prices for the rest of us. Likewise, the fine wine market is relatively small, at around £500m worldwide. On the other hand, fund managers want something that they can sell without a problem, so wine may not in all cases represent the best option. Thus savers who already have a large cellar may stand to benefit the most.

BUBBLING OVER WITH TRIVIA

Champagne is indeed an amazing drink... but did you know:

- A popped Champagne cork can go 62 miles per hour
- You are more likely to be killed by a misfired Champagne cork than by a poisonous spider.
- To obtain a level of 17% alcohol in the world's strongest beer – Samuel Adams' Triple Bock – the brewers use a Champagne yeast.
- There are 49–58 million bubbles in a standard bottle of Champagne.
- When it comes to bubble size, small is beautiful: large bubbles are considered unsightly and are the mark of a lower quality bubbly.
- Contrary to popular belief, Dom Pérignon did not invent Champagne, but he did perfect it – by regulating the second fermentation; by using stronger bottles; by substituting a cork for traditional hemp closure... and he was a very skilled blender.
- Barbe-Nicole Ponsardin Clicquot (the Veuve Clicquot) invented the riddling process, which is used to remove the cloudy mass of dead yeast cells left after fermentation, leaving the liquid crystal-clear. When her husband died in 1805, she took over the Champagne house and was henceforth called Veuve ('Widow') Cliquot.
- The fat molecules in lipstick and greasy snacks like peanuts break the bubble walls, taking the fizz out of Champagne.
- The pressure in a bottle of Champagne is 90 pounds per square inch, about three times that of an automobile tyre – or equivalent to that of the tyre of a double-decker bus (apparently many countries fill their double-decker bus tyres to exactly the same level, as there are multinational claims on this statistic).

IT'S THE WINE TALKING

It is desirable to have a knowledge of true literature, of composition and versifying, of wind and string instruments; and it is well, moreover, to be learned in precedent and court ceremonies, so as to be a model for others. One should write not unskillfully in the running hand, be able to sing in a pleasing voice and keep good time to music; and, lastly, a man should not refuse a little wine when it is pressed upon him.
Yoshida Kenko, Japanese court official and poet (1283–1350)

YOU'VE BEEN BRANDED

Each year, the world's largest wine and spirits companies spend millions, literally, on advertising and promotion to consumers, both in point of sale at supermarkets and wine merchants, and on television – all in an effort to get you to try their wines. The myriad marketing partnerships UK consumers might recognise include that of Jacob's Creek and *Friends* (ended in 2004); Blossom Hill and *Will & Grace*; and Baileys and *Sex & the City*. Not to mention periodic product placements and even inadvertent endorsements, such as Bollinger's starring role on Absolutely Fabulous. But if sponsorship didn't work, companies would take their business elsewhere.

Of the top 20 brands by turnover (year ending May 2005) with which you may be familiar, you'll note that most are owned by a few companies. You'll also note that a French brand doesn't make it into the top 10 – but the French are known more for more upmarket wines so this is understandable.   *(Source: AC Neilsen)*

Brand	Country	Company
Hardys	Australia	Constellation
Blossom Hill	US	Percy Fox
E&J Gallo	US	E&J Gallo
Jacob's Creek	Australia	Pernod Ricard
Kumala	South Africa	Western Wines
Stowells of Chelsea	Several	Constellation
Lindemans	Australia	FGL Wine Estates
Banrock Station	Australia	Constellation
Rosemount	Australia	FGL Wine Estates
Wolf Blass	Australia	FGL Wine Estates
Piat d'Or	France	Percy Fox
Rivercrest	US	E&J Gallo
JPChenet	France	Les Grands Chais de France
Isla Negra	Chile	Western Wines
Echo Falls	US	Constellation
Concha & Toro	Chile	Concha & Toro
Fetzer	US	Brown-Foreman
Namaqua	South Africa	Raisin Social
Paul Masson	US	Constellation
Arniston Bay	South Africa	Omnia

NUMBER-CRUNCHING... AND SIPPING

- The average cost of a French oak barrel is $600 (£336)
- The approximate price of an American oak barrel is $250 (£140)
- There are approximately 300 bottles of wine in a 60-gallon barrel
- There are approximately 600 grapes in a bottle of wine
- There are an estimated 10,000 varieties of wine grapes in the world (many of them related to each other)
- Foot treading of grapes is still used in the production of a small quantity of high quality port
- There are 20 million acres devoted to grapes, worldwide
- There are 5 million yeast cells in one average drop of fermenting grape juice
- There are over 400 species of oak but only 20 are used in barrel making; of these, only 5% are considered suitable for high quality barrels
- The average age of a French oak tree harvested for use in barrels is 170 years

NOUVEAUX PAUVRES

It is hard to explain why otherwise sensible drinkers get caught up in the race for the Beaujolais Nouveau each November. It is by any standard a less than inspiring wine. It has, however, been supported by some canny commercial interests since the 1950s, when a number of merchants in Burgundy recognised the value of a wine that they could sell within a few weeks of the harvest to generate the money needed to buy and store finer wines from the region.

It took off because its seasonality appealed, in particular to urban drinkers, at first with mild interest in the 1960s, leading to the frenzy of a 1974 *Sunday Times* newspaper competition. In that year the Director of Dateline, John Patterson, picked up the released wine in France at midnight on Thursday 14 November and reached the newspaper office at 2.30am on Friday.

This all goes to show that when it comes to matters of the heart and seduction, any old plonk may prove as effective in reaching your goal as the finest grand cru. The producers effectively abolished the race, after dangerous speeding ensued. They decided that the wine was to be released not from Beaujolais, but from the port of Calais at midnight.

Time is fun when you're having flies.

🍷

THROUGH A GLASS DARKLY

When the German word 'trocken' appears on a wine label, what does it mean?

a) dry
b) semi-dry
c) best drunk before...
d) vintage
Answer on page 153.

🍷

IT'S THE WINE TALKING

*What is better than to sit at the end of the day and drink wine
with friends, or substitutes for friends?*
James Joyce

GREAT WINE RECIPES

Beef Bourguignon

This may be a classic, but not everyone can agree what should go into it. We have just two rules when making Beef Bourguignon. Firstly, never use a wine for cooking that you wouldn't happily drink with the meal. In fact, get several bottles, cook with some and accompany this deeply aromatic stew with the others. Secondly, always let it cool and reheat the next day – the flavours are so much more harmonious after a day of steeping together. Also, there is no point making it in tiny quantities for two or even four. Get out some freezer bags if you're not intending to feed a dozen, as it keeps perfectly for several months.

First make your marinade. Roughly chop up a large onion, a large carrot and a couple of sticks of celery, and fry them in olive oil. Add two bottles of good Burgundy, some fresh thyme, four or five bay leaves, a few black pepper corns and a big, juicy head of garlic cut in half horizontally (much quicker than bashing each clove individually). Bring to the boil and let cool.

Cut up four pounds of chuck steak – or, if you can get to France, the special thick cuts of sinewy leg beef sold specifically for Beef Bourguignon – into two-inch cubes, cover with cold marinade and leave in the fridge overnight. When ready the beef will have turned a deep purple colour. Next day strain and reserve the liquid.

Fry an eight ounce piece of smoked bacon or pancetta, or some chopped up bits of bacon, with a pound of whole shallots in a mixture of olive oil and butter until golden. Put in the bottom of a big casserole dish. Add some more oil to the pan, get it very hot, and fry off the pieces of beef, which you've patted dry with a towel, until good and brown. You can dredge them in flour, which thickens the stew, before frying, or you can add it afterwards, mixed in with the marinade. It'll take two or three batches to do them all, but don't crowd the pan. De-glaze the pan with some of the marinade and pour into the casserole.

Add the remains of the marinade to the casserole with half a pint of beef stock. Cover and cook in a low oven (150°C/300°F/Gas mark 2) for about four hours. You won't get away with less than three and extra time doesn't hurt. The meat should be melting. Some people like to enrich it with some brandy. Some like to add fried button mushrooms half way through cooking. Some stick in more chunks of carrot... your choice.

THROUGH A GLASS DARKLY

**If trying to pronounce the world's wine regions twists your tongue enough –
here are some of your favourites, in a new format.**

a) ELITISM NO – hint: the oldest wine-growing area of Bordeaux
b) PAELLA NAVY – hint: the Screaming Eagle flies from here
c) A CLARET GO NOT – hint: Kiwis see gold in their Pinot Noir
d) INEPT MOE – hint: pigs find something heavenly here

Answer on page 153.

WINE TOUR ETIQUETTE

Whether you're in a big winery with scheduled tours and tour guides, or at a small oper-
ation where you've turned up and they've kindly agreed to give you a look at what's
going on, there are some dos and don'ts of polite wine tourism to take on board.

DO be aware of where in the winemaking year you are, which varies from region to
region. At key stages smaller vineyards are less likely to welcome you with open arms
– they're much more concerned with getting the harvest in.

DON'T drink everything in sight if you don't intend buying anything. Vineyards aren't
open to the public as a service, they do it in the hope of selling more wine.

DO let them know your preferences. There's nothing wrong with saying you never
drink whites as it's a waste of everyone's time and their money if they ply you with
samples of something you're never going to buy in a million years.

DON'T be afraid to ask for help. There's nothing shameful about having different
notes pointed out to you

DO be willing to experiment and try some types of wine you either don't know well
or haven't liked before. County, region and even side of the hill can make a hell of a
lot of difference to the taste of the finished wine.

DON'T swallow if you want to taste a large range of wines, or you'll wind up drunk
and unable to appreciate them. In general try and taste lighter wines first, whites
before reds.

FOR MEDICINAL PURPOSES ONLY

There are many references in Homer to blended potions which were used medicinally. When Hector bears the wounded Machaon to his tent, Hecamede mixes what sounds like a disgusting blend of Pramian wine, goats' milk, cheese and barley meal. Presumably kill or cure.

WORDS ON WINE

You may drink to your leman in gold,
In a great golden goblet of wine;
She's as ripe as the wine, and as bold
As the glare of the gold:
But this little lady of mine,
I will not profane her in wine.
I go where the garden so still is
(The moon raining through),
To pluck the white bowls of the lilies,
And drink her in dew!

**Richard Henry Stoddard,
'Wine and Dew' from *Oriental Songs***

NOW *THAT'S* WHAT I CALLED AGED...

Starting in 1952, French undersea explorer Jacques Cousteau (1910–1997) and his team unearthed a couple of shipwrecked vessels, buried under the mud near Grand-Congloué Island, off the coast of Marseilles, France. Dating as far back as the second century BC, the cargo of the first ship apparently included 400 Greco-Roman wine amphorae (containers), while the second ship held about 30 Greek amphorae. Someone inevitably asked him what he did with the wine (thinking that he might have sold it or given it to a museum) and supposedly he said, 'It was delicious.' This story is probably apocryphal, as the wine would certainly have been undrinkable.

But then, he was French...

QUIET FLOWS THE DON

According to *History Today*, rumour has long swirled around the idea of a secret tunnel connecting the wine cellars of the two St John's Colleges in Cambridge and Oxford. Through this tunnel the dons stealthily travel annually for a glass of Madeira underneath the relentlessly depressing and plebeian Stansted airport.

Likely? We think not.

IT'S THE WINE TALKING

Hamlet's mother, she's the queen
Buys it in the final scene
Drinks a glass of funky wine
Now she's Satan's Valentine.
Military marching chant in the film *Renaissance Man* (1994)

OFF WITH HIS HEAD!

Toast drinking could be a political act during the seventeenth century and into the eighteenth, especially if a man was goading the Parliamentarians by drinking a toast to Charles II. After the Restoration, the toast was a mark of royalist loyalty and later, after 1688, there was a choice: toasting the monarch or the Stuart Pretenders.

Violence was never far from the surface here and a man who toasted the wrong side could well end up being beaten up, unless it was in a Jacobite-inclined county such as Denbighshire. There, the greatest magnate Watkyn Williams-Wynn was strongly suspected of being a Jacobite himself and was forced to make a hasty retreat from Shrewsbury in order to avoid charges of drinking toasts to the Pretender.

The political considerations aside, toasting was a serious business in the sixteenth and seventeenth centuries. Some hosts struck the stems from the glasses to ensure continuous drinking, while in Perthshire a rule applied that if a guest failed to empty his glass to a toast he had to drink the same toast a second time from a full glass.

TEN GREAT PRODUCERS OF BIODYNAMIC WINE

Domaine Zind-Humbrecht *(Alsace, France)*

Domaine Leflaive *(Burgundy, France)*

Domaine Leroy *(Burgundy, France)*

Clos de la Coulée de Serrant *(Loire Valley, France)*

Domaine Huet *(Loire Valley, France)*

M Chapoutier *(Rhône Valley, France)*

Domaine Gauby *(Roussillon, France)*

Castello di Argiano *(Tuscany, Italy)*

Fetzer Vineyards *(California, USA)*

Cullen *(Western Australia)*

BURN BABY BURN

The diarist Samuel Pepys, like many prominent men of his age, was a hardened drinker. He frequently drank far too much wine and beer (sometimes mixed!) and was advised by his doctors not to indulge. Among the many incidents Pepys recorded was the Great Fire of 1666, which burnt more than 400 acres of London to the ground. He gave us one of the most vivid eyewitness accounts of the fire: 'Everybody endeavouring to remove their goods, and flinging into the River or bringing them into lighters that lay off. Poor people staying in their houses as long as till the very fire touched them, and then running into boats or clambering from one pair of stairs by the waterside to another. And among other things, the poor pigeons I perceive were loath to leave their houses, but hovered about the windows and balconies till they were some of them burned, their wings, and fell down.'

Pepys observed the fire's progress for a couple of days, and as it grew nearer his house, made preparation for it by burying his most precious belongings (including his wine): 'And did by moonshine (it being brave, dry, and moonshine and warm weather) carry much of my goods into the garden, and Mr. Hater and I did remove my money and iron chests into my cellar, as thinking that the safest place. And got my bags of gold into my office ready to carry away...'

WORDS ON WINE

A large cask of wine had been dropped and broken, in the street. The accident had happened in getting it out of a cart; the cask had tumbled out with a run, the hoops had burst, and it lay on the stones just outside the door of the wine-shop, shattered like a walnut-shell.

All the people within reach had suspended their business, or their idleness, to run to the spot and drink the wine. The rough, irregular stones of the street, pointing every way, and designed, one might have thought, expressly to lame all living creatures that approached them, had dammed it into little pools; these were surrounded, each by its own jostling group or crowd, according to its size. Some men kneeled down, made scoops of their two hands joined, and sipped, or tried to help women, who bent over their shoulders, to sip, before the wine had all run out between their fingers. Others, men and women, dipped in the puddles with little mugs of mutilated earthenware, or even with handkerchiefs from women's heads, which were squeezed dry into infants' mouths; others made small mud-embankments, to stem the wine as it ran; others, directed by lookers-on up at high windows, darted here and there, to cut off little streams of wine that started away in new directions; others devoted themselves to the sodden and lee-dyed pieces of the cask, licking, and even champing the moister wine-rotted fragments with eager relish. There was no drainage to carry off the wine, and not only did it all get taken up, but so much mud got taken up along with it, that there might have been a scavenger in the street, if anybody acquainted with it could have believed in such a miraculous presence.

The wine was red wine, and had stained the ground of the narrow street in the suburb of Saint Antoine, in Paris, where it was spilled. It had stained many hands, too, and many faces, and many naked feet, and many wooden shoes. The hands of the man who sawed the wood, left red marks on the billets; and the forehead of the woman who nursed her baby, was stained with the stain of the old rag she wound about her head again. Those who had been greedy with the staves of the cask, had acquired a tigerish smear about the mouth; and one tall joker so besmirched, his head more out of a long squalid bag of a nightcap than in it, scrawled upon a wall with his finger dipped in muddy wine-lees – BLOOD.

**Charles Dickens, *A Tale of Two Cities*
(1859)**

VINI - CULTURE

We know wine makes ordinary people want to sing... even more so when it plays a role in an opera. Here are a few operas in which wine is sometimes a Diva, sometimes a bit player... but always on the tongue.

L'Incontro Improvviso (Haydn)
Falstaff (Verdi)
The Rake's Progress (Stravinsky)
Die tote Stadt (Korngold)
Faust (Gounod)
Die Fledermaus (Strauss)
Der Rosenkavalier (Strauss)
Nozze Istriane (Smareglia)
Otello (Verdi)
L'Amico Fritz (Mascagni)
Iolanta (Tchaikovsky)
Rigoletto (Verdi)
Don Giovanni (Mozart)
La Cenerentola (Rossini)
Cavelleria Rusticana (Mascagni)
Billy Budd (Britten)

THE GRAPES OF RAP

Like the Tsars of Russia, today's rap music stars are partial to Cristal Champagne (Roederer). As Mis-teeq sings in her song *One Night Stand*, 'Act wild but I got style/ 'Cos I ain't sipping if it ain't Cristal'. Rapper 50 Cent sings in *Rotten Apple*, 'I play the bar with eight bottles all night gettin' right/Teachin' the hoodrats what Cristal taste like'. Similarly, LL Cool J has rapped about Hennessy Cognac, and Busta Rhymes and P Diddy shouted 'Give me the Henny, you can give me the Cris/You can pass me the Remy, but then pass the Courvoisier' in their tune Pass the Courvoisier.

Doesn't rhyme, exactly, but it does go down nice and smooth...

GODS OF THE GRAPE

Before the Romans arrived in Italy and set up their civilisation, borrowing gods from the Greeks, the earlier Italian tribes had their own gods and goddesses, including Liber and Libera. Although they came to be associated with plenty and wine, the original gods were probably rather different. Scholars think Liber was a god of masculinity and ejaculation – certainly he had a phallic cult worshipping him in Lavinium, who would cart around a giant penis and, during his festival, install it in the forum and crown it with floral wreaths. The festival of Liber and Libera was 17 March, and this was the day 17-year-old Roman youths would officially be declared men. As Liber's female counterpart, Libera was a goddess of female fertility, and her temple features statues of female genitalia. Some depictions of her show her crowned with ivy, carrying an ivy-twined spear, and holding a bunch of grapes. A further cult, with Ceres, the goddess of corn and harvest, worshiped them as the Aventine Triad during the early republic, and associated them with the Greek Demeter, Dionysos and Persephone. The cult of the Aventine Triad was particularly politicised and provided a focal point for plebeian class consciousness.

LA LA LA LA LA AMERICA!

- A British writer once said that the US makes the loveliest wines in the world and don't realise it; he also said that calling them 'domestic' was enough to start trouble anywhere

- The average American drinks about one tenth the wine of an average French person

- Nearly 50% of all the wine imported into the US is Italian, and 25% is French

- The US has over 3,300 wineries

- Wine is made in every State, but commercial wine is made in 48 States

- Ninety percent of all American wine is made in California

- Prior to the US Civil War (1861–1865), Ohio was considered America's most important wine producing State

- The nineteenth-century American poet, Henry Wadsworth Longfellow, mentions wine more than 300 times in his works.

- California, unsurprisingly, has the most 'bricks and mortar' wineries (over 1,300) followed by Washington State (300); Oregon (200+) New York (167) and Pennsylvania (93)

THE METHUEN TREATY

There was widespread smuggling of French wine and Champagne in the eighteenth century, as the English had developed a taste for these fine wines at the end of the previous century. Port, however, was universally held in low esteem until Queen Anne tried to thrust it upon people with the 1703 Methuen Treaty with Portugal, when rates of duty at £7 per tun (252 gallons) were imposed on Portuguese wines as opposed to £55 per tun on French.

Thereafter, nothing much changed. Queen Anne ordered a token amount of Port but continued to prefer French claret, burgundy, Champagne and Hermitage and smuggling – even by some of her own courtiers, like Lady Sutherland who had to pay over £250 in fines after one Dutch foray – continued unabated until 1768. This was the year that William Pitt the Younger transferred the greater part of the wine duty from Customs to Excise. This meant that once the wine landed, the duty had to be paid in any event and thus people who wished to drink French wines had little choice but to pay the exorbitant level of duty.

WORDS ON WINE

In the time of Henry VIII, wine was used at breakfast and even the grave Sir Thomas More drank frequent bumpers* in the morning before proceeding to state business. This learned statesman is recorded the following anecdote: Sir Thomas More was sent by Henry VIII as Ambassador to a foreign court. The morning he was to have his audience, knowing the virtue of wine, he ordered his servant to bring him a large glass of Sack**, and having drank that, he called for another.

The servant with officious ignorance would have dissuaded him from a second draught but in vain. The Ambassador drank off a second and demanded a third which he also drained, insisting on a fourth. He was persuaded by his servant to let it alone. He then went to his audience. When however he returned home, he called for his servant and threatened him with his cane. 'You rogue', said he, 'what have you done me? I spoke so to the Emperor on the inspiration of those three first glasses that I drank, that he told me I was fit to govern three parts of the world. Now you dog, if I had drank the fourth glass, I had been fit to govern all the world.'

*Bumper: a drinking cup filled to the brim – used for toasting, especially departures.
** Sherry

Charles Tovey, *Wit, Wisdom and Morals, Distilled from Bacchus* (1878)

WORDS ON WINE

Three cups of wine a prudent man may take:
The first of them for constitution's sake;
The second to the girl he loves the best;
The third and last to lull him to his rest
Then home to bed. But if a fourth he pours
That is the cup of folly and not ours
Loud noisy talking on the fifth attends
The six breeds feuds and falling out of friends
Seven begets blows and faces stained with gore
Eight and the watch patrol breaks ope the door;
Mad with the ninth, another cup goes round,
And the swilled sot drops senseless on the ground.

Charles Tovey, *Wit, Wisdom and Morals, Distilled from Bacchus* (1878).
(NB This poem has also been attributed to English philosopher Richard Cumberland.)

IT'S THE WINE TALKING

Three be the things I shall never attain: envy, content and sufficient Champagne.
Dorothy Parker, American humourist

FIRST CATCH YOUR RAT...

For competitive macho drinkers rat wine is an obvious purchase, if you can find it. Having eaten the worm from countless bottles of mescal you have to move up a stage, and drinking wine in which baby rats have been steeping sounds like an interesting challenge. The wine originates in Southern China, where they produce a multitude of medicinal wine tonics featuring creatures that sound distinctly off-putting to a western audience. Rat foetuses are put into large bottles that are filled up with rice wine, then left to mature, usually for five years or upwards. If kept for a long period delicate body parts like tails and toes do tend to rot off and float around the wine, which is amber coloured and tastes like a less rich version of Madeira. It's drunk after meals as a general tonic and is supposed to guard against arthritis.

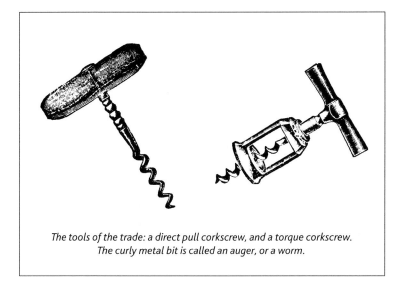

The tools of the trade: a direct pull corkscrew, and a torque corkscrew.
The curly metal bit is called an auger, or a worm.

SWIMMING IN CHAMPERS

What says romance like a seven-foot Champagne glass whirlpool bath for two? Well, nothing, according to Caesars Pocono Resorts, who offer a suite in the Roman Towers complete with the lavish bath, a separate heart-shaped pool, a round king-size bed with celestial ceiling, plus a cosy log-burning fireplace, massage table and dry sauna.

Set on Pocono Palace's golf course, the Roman Towers are designed on a grand Roman theme, with a contemporary living room featuring floor to ceiling Corinthian columns, arches, eighteen-foot high vaulted ceilings, covered walkways and a private, arched underpass for parking. In addition, a cathedral window offers a panoramic view of the Pocono Palace's lush surrounding landscape.

The only problem might be to convince your partner that swimming in water, rather than the many bottles of Champagne required to actually fill the seven-foot glass, might be just as romantic and not at all cheapskate.

63

WINE WORDS

Fiasco

Italian for 'flask', the word most often associated with the short, round-based, straw baskets that cover bottles of inexpensive Chianti and make kitsch souvenir candle-holders. The straw covering helps the bottle stay upright and protects the fragile glass. There are different theories on why the same word for flask/bottle has come to mean disaster. One traces the word's roots to Italian theatre, where the term 'fare fiasco' (literally, to make a bottle) described the act of messing up one's lines, leading to embarrassment in front of an audience. It's possible that 'fiasco' referred to an actual accident on-stage, such as dropping a bottle. Another theory traces the phrase 'fare fiasco' to Italian glass-blowers who would, if they made a mistake when making an ornate item, set it aside for future use in making a flask or bottle.

THROUGH A GLASS DARKLY

**What colour are the following wines, and just to be bit meaner –
what colour are the grapes used to make them?**
(Hint: white wine can be made from red grapes, but not the reverse…)

a) White Zinfandel
b) Champagne
c) Pinot Gris
d) Port
Answer on page 154.

I COULD DIE HAPPY

They say you should be careful what you wish for. In the case of Sam Davidovich, enjoying wine too much led to his downfall. In December 1976, according to the *Daily Mirror*, the 60 year old was in a restaurant in Tel Aviv, enjoying a glass of wine as the band played his favourite song. 'This is how I want to die,' he's reported as saying, 'with a glass of wine in my hand while the band plays my tune.' Moments later he was romantically dancing with his wife to the song when he had a heart attack and dropped dead.

ERSTWHILE VINOUS VOCAB

Terms that have fallen from favour (but perhaps shouldn't have…)

Tappit-hen: A double magnum. A magnum of wine is two quarts; a tappit-hen of wine or rum is a double magnum; a jeroboam of wine or rum is a double tappit-hen; and a rehoboam is a double jeroboam.

Comet Wine: A term of praise for wine of superior quality. A notion prevails that the grapes in comet years are better than in other years, either because the weather is warmer and they ripen better, or because the comets themselves exercise some chemical influence on them. Thus, wine of the years 1811, 1826, 1839, 1845, 1852, 1858, 1861, have a repute. Usage: 'The old gentleman yet nurses some few bottles of the famous comet year (ie 1811), emphatically called comet wine.' – *The Times*

Good Wine Needs no Bush: It was customary to hang out ivy, boughs of trees, flowers etc at public house to notify travellers that 'good cheer' might be had within. Usage: 'Some ale-houses upon the road I saw, And some bushes showing they wine did draw.' – Poor Robin's *Perambulations* (1678)

Source: Brewer's Dictionary of Phrase and Fable *(1898)*

SOUR GRAPES: FROM WINE TO VINEGAR

Grapes bring two types of yeasts to the vat – wild yeasts and wine yeasts. The wild yeasts begin the process of fermentation but they are weak and cannot survive a concentration of over 4% alcohol, so the wine yeasts take over the half-finished job. They are able to raise the alcoholic content of the vat as high as 16%, although it is pretty unusual for there to be that much sugar and the average European percentage is more like 10%.

Then, the wine must be taken from the vat. If it is not, the vinegar bacteria will attack the alcohol, convert it into acetic acid and turn the residue into vinegar. Eventually, the acetic acid will be attacked by the bacteria that have survived, and all that will remain will be water and ammonium salts.

CHAMPAGNE CHARLIES

*There comes a time in every woman's life when the only thing that helps is
a glass of Champagne.*
Bette Davis in *Old Acquaintance* (1943)

*Burgundy makes you think of silly things; Bordeaux makes you talk about them, and
Champagne makes you do them.*
Jean-Anthelme Brillat-Savarin

Come quickly, I am tasting the stars!'
Dom Pérignon

I'm only a beer teetotaller, not a Champagne teetotaller.
George Bernard Shaw

*Before I was born my mother was in great agony of spirit and in a tragic situation. She
could take no food except iced oysters and Champagne. If people ask me when I
began to dance, I reply, 'In my mother's womb, probably as a result of the oysters and
Champagne – the food of Aphrodite.'*
Isadora Duncan

*Champagne's funny stuff. I'm used to whiskey. Whiskey is a slap on the back, and
Champagne's a heavy mist before my eyes.*
Jimmy Stewart in *The Philadelphia Story* (1940)

WHEN MARTINIS JUST AREN'T DE RIGUEUR

Bond's wines: Veuve Cliquot

One can imagine James Bond having flirted outrageously with the newly widowed
27-year-old queen of Champagne, Barbe-Nicole Ponsardin Clicquot – la 'Veuve'
('Widow'). In the book *Casino Royale* (1963), Bond drinks half a bottle of Clicquot to
celebrate his baccarat win, and later orders two bottles in the night-club. Likewise, in
the novel *Diamonds Are Forever* (1956), Bond and love interest-du-moment Tiffany
Case drink Clicquot Rosé in the 21 Club in New York.

WORDS ON WINE

BACCHUS must now his power resign—
I am the only God of Wine!
It is not fit the wretch should be
In competition set with me,
Who can drink ten times more than he.

Make a new world, ye powers divine!
Stock'd with nothing else but Wine:
Let Wine its only product be,
Let Wine be earth, and air, and sea—
And let that Wine be all for me!

Henry Carey (1693–1743), *A Drinking-Song*

YOU'LL NEED A STIFF ONE HERE

A quick glance at the details of Chateau Ste Michelle, Washington State's founding winery at 14111 Northeast 145th Street, Woodinville, reveals award-winning wines and a wine tasting experience second to none, as the winery uses some of the best vineyards in the state such as Cold Creek, Canoe Ridge Estate and Horse Heaven to supply its grapes.

But there's more, much more, to Chateau Ste Michelle. The 150 acre winery was previously owned by Seattle lumber and dairy baron Frederick Stimson and his turn of the century mansion is said to be haunted. The 'ghost' is a young girl that Stimson allegedly got pregnant. She suffered an accident on the back stairwell leading to the kitchen and ever since there has been a reputed range of supernatural occurences at the house. Reported activity includes: cold spots that follow you; strange shadows and noises; the feeling of the dead mistress's presence in the upper rooms; unexplained opening and closing of doors and windows, and lights turning on and off.

Of course it may just be the possibility of experiencing all of this, plus the mystery footsteps pattering down the landings and toilets flushing on and off without warning that makes visitors sign up for the grand tour.

TEMPER, TEMPER

The Temperance Movement was a formal endeavour on the part of various religious, social and political interest groups, starting in the early nineteenth century, to encourage abstinence from alcohol. 'Temperance' actually means moderation – which few would argue against. And while some in the movement actually did help develop formal support and services for alcoholics, many proponents of the Temperance Movement misappropriated the term and urged complete teetotalism for all. In fact it was political pressure from the most strident voices that led to Prohibition in the US. But the movement wasn't confined to the US by any means. There were literally thousands of temperance societies around the world. A very few include:

● The Knights of Father Matthew. Founded in Cork, Ireland, in 1838, the movement attracted somewhere over six million followers; some members had 'KFM'; 'K of FM' or LAKFM (Ladies Auxiliary of the Knights of Father Matthew) engraved on their headstones

● The Washingtonian movement. Launched the same year as the Knights of Father Matthew, the Washingtonians were a group of four alcoholics who met in a bar in Baltimore, Maryland. They felt that by exchanging their experiences and anxieties, and by depending on each other (and on religion), they could achieve sobriety. They pre-dated Alcoholics Anonymous by a century.

● The International Organisation of Good Templars. Founded in 1851, the IOGT is a global community of non-governmental organisations that aims to help people live freer and more rewarding lives, without alcohol and other drugs. All members are entitled to personal freedom and must work to improve the quality of life for all; the group advocates democracy and peaceful settlement of conflicts between individuals and groups.

● The Aberystwyth Auxiliary Temperance Society. This was formed in 1835 as a response to the Beer Law (1830) which allowed any taxpayer to pay two guineas a year and open a beer house, leading to a significant increase in the number of public houses

● The Going-Snake District Temperance Society, founded 1844. From the records of the Cherokee Messenger: 'dark clouds of intemperance had assumed an unusually threatening aspect; the friends of Temperance felt that something must be done, but almost despaired of success, while the cause of all this mischief, a single grog shop, was in the way. But that evil curate itself, a young man, now the Secretary of the Society, had the hardihood to relinquish the intoxicating cup himself, and to make the first effort.'

● The Valontuote Temperance Society of Minnesota, US. Organised in 1893 and affiliated with the Finnish National Temperance Brotherhood in America, in 1897 it left this organisation because of a dispute over a rule against dancing. The Valontuote merged with the Nuori Suomi Temperance Societies and remained in existence until 1966.

IT'S THE WINE TALKING

I'd rather have a free bottle in front of me than a pre-frontal lobotomy.
Tom Waits, gravel-voiced singer/songwriter

TRAVAIL A L'ANGLAISE

In a botched eighteenth century marketing exercise, producers of claret adulterated it to make it taste as much as possible like Port by the method known as the *travail à l'anglaise.*

After the harvest, a stronger wine from a warmer climate was added to the claret together with some wine whose fermentation had been arrested before all the sugar had turned to alcohol, otherwise known as stum wine. Occasionally, brandy was added.

As a result, the claret re-fermented and became more alcoholic. If it was a great claret, stronger wines from the Rhône valley might be added. For lesser clarets, wines from Alicante in Spain might be used instead.

In any case, all French growers despaired of being forced to such a stratagem by the English palate which was deemed unable to appreciate any finesse or delicacy of bouquet and for whom a strong and rough wine was by definition a good wine.

69

'She gets the Bentley and the house on Eton
Square, and I get the Mouton '45.'

WINE WORDS

Kir

A lovely, refreshing drink made with white wine (preferably aligoté, from Burgundy) and crème de cassis (blackcurrant liqueur), the Kir is named after the former mayor of Dijon, Canon Félix Kir (1876–1968). His burst of inspiration came from the impetus to promote both wine and cassis, the two critical products of the region. The same drink made with sparkling wine – such as a Crémant de Bourgogne or Champagne – is known as a Kir Royale.

IT'S THE WINE TALKING

I can certainly see that you know your wine. Most of the guests who stay here wouldn't know the difference between Bordeaux and Claret.
Basil Fawlty, *Fawlty Towers*

ARE THEY TALKING ABOUT US?

The wine industry defines its typical wine-buying customers as follows. Which one are you?

Mainstream at-homers: Comprising 42% of wine drinkers, they are suburb-based – or rural – parents aged 35–54. They drink about three times a week at home, and spend £4–£5 per bottle. Their favourites are French, Chilean, Australian, South African. They enjoy learning about wine, and are influenced by promotions.

Weekly treaters: 18% of wine drinkers are single, aged 18–34, and drink wine once a week or less. They consider wine 'aspirational' but aren't very interested, and spend about £5 per bottle. They focus on price and familiarity with a brand and tend to drink Australian, German and Italian.

Adventurous connoisseurs: 20% of wine drinkers are very involved and interested in wine, spend a lot and consider themselves sophisticated consumers. Usually from high-income families, they read the critics' columns in up-market publications. They spend £6–£7 per bottle bought for home consumption, three times a week; their tastes are varied but they are particularly interested in red wine; Champagne; Port; and also favour New Zealand and Portugal. They often eat at restaurants, travel widely, and are not usually attracted by promotions.

Sociable bargain hunters: 10% of wine drinkers rely heavily on price and promotion. They'll spend an average of £3.50–£4 a bottle. With children out of the house, they read middle-market tabloid papers, enjoy eating out and are somewhat interested in learning about wine. They'll try wine from a wide variety of countries – as long as it doesn't break the bank.

Frugal conservatives: 10% of wine drinkers are from low-income households, they drink once a week or less, mainly white wine from France and Spain. They'll spend between £3.50 and £4 a bottle and are usually not very interested in trying new things.

GODS OF THE GRAPE

Although people tend to associate Hinduism with not drinking, many Hindu sects do not ban it. So long as alcohol is consumed in moderation it's considered quite acceptable. In the Vedas, the ancient primary texts of Hinduism composed between 1500BC and 600BC, there is even a Hindu goddess of wine, called Sura. Admittedly she's not one of the more important deities, but at least wine gets a representative.

BEST BURGUNDY VINTAGES OF THE LAST 100 YEARS

2002	1999	1995
1990	1985	1978
1971	1969	1966
1964	1959	1949
1945	1937	1929

WORDS ON WINE

There was a table set out under a tree in front of the house, and the March Hare and the Hatter were having tea at it: a Dormouse was sitting between them, fast asleep, and the other two were using it as a cushion, resting their elbows on it, and talking over its head. 'Very uncomfortable for the Dormouse,' thought Alice; 'only, as it's asleep, I suppose it doesn't mind.'

The table was a large one, but the three were all crowded together at one corner of it: 'No room! No room!' they cried out when they saw Alice coming. 'There's PLENTY of room!' said Alice indignantly, and she sat down in a large arm-chair at one end of the table.

'Have some wine,' the March Hare said in an encouraging tone.

Alice looked all round the table, but there was nothing on it but tea. 'I don't see any wine,' she remarked.

'There isn't any,' said the March Hare.

'Then it wasn't very civil of you to offer it,' said Alice angrily.

'It wasn't very civil of you to sit down without being invited,' said the March Hare.

'I didn't know it was YOUR table,' said Alice; 'it's laid for a great many more than three.'

Lewis Carroll, *Alice's Adventures in Wonderland* (1865)

THROUGH A GLASS DARKLY

What is Muscadet?

a) the surname of a pioneering French oenologist

b) a type of barrel used to age wines in the Loire region

c) the name of a wine, a grape, and a region

d) a new wine from the producer of Mouton Cadet

Answer on page 154.

FULL OF FLAVOUR

Perhaps surprisingly, all the usual additives used in standard winemaking – sulphur; gelatine; egg whites and so on – are permitted in wine that is biodynamically produced, as long as they are not genetically modified products. Where biodynamic production differs most from standard production is in the composts used in the vineyard. For example, you might find the following in biodynamic compost:

Yarrow

Camomile

Stinging nettles

Oak bark

Dandelion

Valerian

A cow horn filled with cow manure

FILL YOUR BOOTS

Beau Brummel, the most notorious dandy of the Regency period, used to say that his valet used best Champagne to get the pristine shine on his Hessian boots, which was much envied by his contemporaries. Certainly valets at the period used all manner of things to try and produce the brightest shine on leather, but there are no actual recipes. What do exist, however, are several rather cross letters and diaries of young men who wished afterwards they'd drunk their Champagne rather than handing it over to the servants for cleaning purposes.

IT'S THE WINE TALKING

Good wine ruins the purse; bad wine ruins the stomach.
Spanish proverb

WORDS ON WINE

Plenty of dust comes in at Mr Tulkinghorn's windows, and plenty more has generated among his furniture and papers. It lies thick everywhere. When a breeze from the country that has lost its way takes fright and makes a blind hurry to rush out again, it flings as much dust in the eyes of Allegory as the law – or Mr Tulkinghorn, one of its trustiest representatives – may scatter, on occasion, in the eyes of the laity.

In his lowering magazine of dust, the universal article into which his papers and himself, and all his clients, and all things of earth, animate and inanimate, are resolving, Mr Tulkinghorn sits at one of the open windows enjoying a bottle of old Port. Though a hard-grained man, close, dry, and silent, he can enjoy old wine with the best. He has a priceless binn of Port in some artful cellar under the Fields, which is one of his many secrets. When he dines alone in chambers, as he has dined to-day, and has his bit of fish and his steak or chicken brought in from the coffee-house, he descends with a candle to the echoing regions below the deserted mansion, and heralded by a remote reverberation of thundering doors, comes gravely back encircled by an earthy atmosphere and carrying a bottle from which he pours a radiant nectar, two score and ten years old, that blushes in the glass to find itself so famous and fills the whole room with the fragrance of southern grapes.

Mr Tulkinghorn, sitting in the twilight by the open window, enjoys his wine. As if it whispered to him of its fifty years of silence and seclusion, it shuts him up the closer. More impenetrable than ever, he sits, and drinks, and mellows as it were in secrecy; pondering, at that twilight hour, on all the mysteries he knows, associated with darkening woods in the country, and vast blank shut-up houses in town; and perhaps sparing a thought or two for himself, and his family history, and his money, and his will – all a mystery to every one – and that one bachelor friend of his, a man of the same mould and a lawyer too, who lived the same kind of life until he was seventy-five years old, and then, suddenly conceiving (as it is supposed) an impression that it was too monotonous, gave his gold watch to his hair-dresser one summer evening, and walked leisurely home to the Temple, and hanged himself.

Charles Dickens, *Bleak House* (1852–3)

HEROIC DRUNKS

Charles Bukowski (1920-1994)

Never let the doctors tell you that a bottle of red wine doesn't equal a prolific literary output. Charles Bukowski, a Los Angeles poet and novelist, wrote an extraordinary 50 books before his death on 9 March, 1994 – all rocket-fuelled by drink. A product of a dysfunctional Great Depression childhood punctuated by ritualistic razor strop beatings administered by his father, Bukowski's lifelong feelings of isolation contributed to his struggles with alcoholism. His achievement is all the more extraordinary, because he didn't become a writer until the age of 49, after an early adulthood working odd jobs and roaming across the United States.

He worked for 11 years for the United States Postal Service in Los Angeles, which forms the basis of his first and gentlest book. It wasn't until 1969 that Bukowski decided to make writing his full-time career. As he explained in a letter at the time, 'I have one of two choices: stay in the post office and go crazy... or stay out here and play at writer and starve. I have decided to starve.'

One critic described Bukowski's fiction as a 'detailed depiction of a certain taboo male fantasy: the uninhibited bachelor, slobby, anti-social, and utterly free,' and his reputation as a wine-consuming machine certainly played its part. Staving off creditors and hunger pangs with cheap liquor, he manfully wrote in the novel *Ham on Rye*: 'I decided that I would always like getting drunk. It took away the obvious and maybe if you could get away from the obvious often enough, you wouldn't become obvious yourself.'

CHRYSANTHEMUM WINE

In Japan chrysanthemum wine is a special year-old brew drunk to celebrate the Chung Yeung Festival, or Elder's Day. Japanese culture reveres the elderly, and Japanese people used to spend the day visiting the graves of their dead ancestors and going hiking to find dogwood flowers. The wine is supposed to cure many sicknesses and bring a long life, especially if drunk at the top of a hill under a dogwood tree. Chrysanthemums are in their finest bloom during the ninth month of the Japanese calendar when the festival falls, and are particularly highly regarded by the Japanese for their beauty.

BOTTLES VERBOTEN

During much of the seventeenth century it was illegal in England to sell wine in glass bottles. Vintners kept wine in barrels, and people brought their own bottles in to be filled. Glass had become much more widely available thanks to the replacement of charcoal with coal in the glass-blowing industry in the early part of the century. These bottles were closed using bits of wood or cork pushed part way into the opening and tied to the neck, with the lip of the bottle serving to keep them in place. They did nothing to preserve the wine.

IS IT KOSHER?

Wine looms large in Jewish history and tradition – but most observant Jews will likely tell you that the kosher wine they have drunk at weddings, bar mitzvahs and holy days has been pretty awful. That's because, ironically, most kosher wine has been made and handled by non-Jews. Called 'mevushal', in order for it to pass muster the wine has to be heated to 185°F, which gives it a distinct flavour. Also, wine producers such as Manischewitz have made their wine from Concord grapes (traditionally, a table grape), and have vastly over-sweetened them.

Until relatively recently, nobody bothered to make a good kosher wine – or a good wine kosher, for that matter. However demand, for high quality, well-made wine that just happens to be Kosher is on the rise, and producers like Capçanes (in Montsant, Spain) are making excellent wine that anyone would rate highly.

For wine to be considered kosher (meaning 'proper' in Yiddish), it has to be made under the supervision of a Rabbi – and in accordance with Jewish dietary laws. The process starts in the vineyard, where grapes used to make the wine must be at least four years old (which makes sense anyway, as newly planted vines normally require a few years before they yield their best fruit). The vines must be isolated from other fruits and vegetables (ie no other produce may be grown next to or between the vines). In the winery itself, cleanliness is of utmost importance: only kosher ingredients (including bacteria, fining agents, yeasts, etc) may be used – and must be kept completely separate from non-Kosher items. The equipment and tools must be used exclusively for kosher wine, and the winemaker may not add artificial colouring or preservatives. L'chaim!

WHAT'S YOUR MEASURE?

One cluster	**=**	**approximately one glass**
85 grapes	=	one cluster
six clusters	**=**	**one bottle**
40 clusters	=	one vine
one vine	**=**	**10 bottles**
1,200 clusters	=	one barrel
one barrel	**=**	**60 gallons**
60 gallons	=	25 cases
30 vines	**=**	**one barrel**
400 vines	=	one acre
one acre	**=**	**five tonnes**
five tonnes	=	332 cases
one case	**=**	**12 bottles**
12 bottles	=	approximately 48 glasses

NB: some of these are extremely approximate! Obviously winemakers control everything, starting with the number of grapes and leaves on a bunch... which will influence the rest.

AND SOMETHING FOR THE LADIES

While Elizabethan ladies were supping beer with the best of them, by Georgian times women didn't drink very much, if at all. Sherry and Madeira were for older women and Port was generally for men, leaving Champagne punch as a possible drink for the young ladies, as long as there was not a hint of poor behaviour or drunkenness.

By Queen Anne's day, women customarily drank Port and Sherry and meals were finished off with a glass of wine for everyone, following on from dessert wine for the ladies and wine with previous courses. But following Queen Victoria's accession to the throne drinking was frowned upon even more for women, although many discovered that they could enjoy laudanum (opium in water) for a whole range of female ailments instead. Otherwise, the best they could hope for was the sickly almond-scented Orgeat Syrup, made with rosewater, almonds, sugar and oranges, or Ratafia, another almond-flavoured cordial, mixed with water.

LUNCHEON

TO

Celebrate the Publication

OF

The Forbidden Territory

BY

Dennis Wheatley,

IN THE CELLARS OF

Messrs. JUSTERINI & BROOKS,
Wine Merchants,

TO THE ROYAL HOUSE OF ENGLAND
FROM THE REIGN OF KING GEORGE III.

TUESDAY, 3rd JANUARY 1933

THE ARCHES,   VILLIERS STREET,
                                      STRAND.

*From a book launch luncheon in 1933 held at Justerini & Brooks
(wine merchants which still exist today) for Dennis Wheatley,
a writer of thrillers and mysteries.*

THROUGH A GLASS DARKLY

In which of the following is the Sémillon grape not used?
a) White wine from the Graves region of Bordeaux
b) Sauternes (the delectable sweet wine of Bordeaux)
c) Unoaked wines from the Hunter Valley in New South Wales, Australia
d) Late-harvest wines from Madeira
Answer on page 154.

IT'S THE WINE TALKING

Wine is one of the most civilised things in the world and one of the natural things of the world that has been brought to the greatest perfection, and it offers a greater range for enjoyment and appreciation than, possibly, any other purely sensory thing which may be purchased.
Ernest Hemingway, from *Death in the Afternoon* (1932)

WHEN IN ROME

Only the very rich could afford to over indulge in ancient Rome, and even then most banquets were rather quieter affairs than you might think. The style of dining, with three couches each taking three people around three sides of a serving table, meant that most people were satisfied with eight guests for dinner. A rich man might entertain 17 people seated at two tables but more than that was reserved for very special occasions. People saved getting drunk until all the courses had been consumed. The Romans only had three courses, but they often consisted of several dishes, and satirical writings of the day describe guests fasting for days before a banquet to make the most of the free food, and shoveling dishes into their napkins, which where then sent off with a servant back to their house, another source of free meals.

In order to eat and drink huge quantities at feasts, the Romans favoured the emetic antimony, which was fashioned into little goblets that would then be filled with wine and left to ferment on the banqueting table. When the bloated revellers had drunk and eaten too much, they would take a swig from the usually poisonous antimony cup and throw up the lot, thus making room, charmingly, for the next course, disgorging the poison along with the food and drink.

If you didn't fancy getting drunk at a dinner party, you could head for a tavern which were plentiful, cheerful and cheap. Some two hundred taverns have been identified in Pompeii; near the public baths, eight line a single street. Pliny described how the Pompeians would work up a thirst by going to the baths, getting so hot they sometimes became unconscious, then running out to grab a vessel of wine at the nearest wine shop and down it in one, often only to vomit it up and repeat the process.

WORDS ON WINE

Hail, high Excess especially in wine,
To thee in worship do I bend the knee
Who preach abstemiousness unto me
My skull thy pulpit, as my paunch thy shrine.
Precept on precept, aye, and line on line,
Could ne'er persuade so sweetly to agree
With reason as thy touch, exact and free,
Upon my forehead and along my spine.
At thy command eschewing pleasure's cup,
With the hot grape I warm no more my wit;
When on thy stool of penitence I sit
I'm quite converted, for I can't get up.
Ungrateful he who afterward would falter
To make new sacrifices at thine altar!

Ambrose Bierce, *The Devil's Dictionary* (1911)

FOR MEDICINAL PURPOSES ONLY

The Egyptians didn't use wine much in medical treatments, mostly because it was so expensive, beyond the purse of ordinary people. Commoners and slaves in Ancient Egypt did have access to medicine, and the Egyptian employer wasn't unfamiliar with the concept of sick days either. The Egyptians have handed down to us the earliest prescriptions, and seem to have been, like medieval Europeans, obsessed with their digestive system. Among the very first prescriptions is one for a cleansing enema given by a physician described as the doctor of the royal bottom.

One prescription that does involve wine (probably because the poor couldn't afford vanity) is for 'How it can be prevent the falling out of hair', found on a papyrus fragment from the end of the third century BC at Magna Ermoupolis in Middle-Egypt. Resin is mixed with new, sour wine and kneaded together. Myrrh and more wine are added to make a spreadable paste, which is plastered on the head before and after you wash. If anyone tries it (successfully or otherwise) do let us know!

GREAT WINE RECIPES

Eggs poached in red wine

Visually striking, this is essentially poached eggs with rich wine sauce, known as *Oeufs en meurette* in France. The trick is they're poached in the wine that makes the sauce before serving.

For a snack for six or a lunch for three take a bottle of red wine and heat in a frying pan or other wide saucepan until just bubbling. Slip the eggs into the simmering wine one at a time and poach for about five minutes. Remove the eggs (now a purple colour!) and drain them. Add salt and pepper, chopped parsley and a sprig of thyme to the wine, along with a large sliced onion, a finely sliced stick of celery and a finely sliced carrot. While the sauce is cooking toast six pieces of bread in the oven slowly, then rub them with garlic. Ignore recipes which tell you to fry the bread, you've already got a rich dish with an unctuous sauce, deep-fried bread doesn't add anything to the mix.

When the sauce has simmered for 20–25 minutes thicken with one ounce of butter mixed with one tablespoon of flour, slowly whisking this paste into the wine sauce. If it looks too thick, thin with a little beef stock. Meanwhile fry some lardons (small strips of thick-cut bacon) in another pan and strain the sauce, now brown and glossy, over them. Warm the poached eggs by dropping into boiling water for a minute, rest on top of a warm piece of toast, and top with the deep brown sauce.

THE TRICKY WAYS OF TRICKY DICK

According to his biographers, US President Richard Nixon – who fancied himself something of a wine buff – was not above pulling a fast one on his guests by giving them inferior wine while helping himself to the good stuff. In *The Final Days*, Bob Woodward and Carl Bernstein describe an evening when Nixon was entertaining Congressmen on board his yacht, the *Sequoia*. Beef tenderloin was on the menu, and the yacht was well-stocked with Nixon's favourite wine – 1966 Château Margaux which at the time cost about $30 a bottle. Nixon always drank this with beef, and he had given special orders to his stewards regarding what to do when large groups of Congressmen were dining aboard: they were to serve his guests a decent $6 wine, while filling his own glass from a bottle of Château Margaux, wrapped in a towel to conceal the label.

SOPS-IN-WINE

The clove carnation (*Dianthus caryophyllus*) goes by the common name of sops-in-wine because it was supposed that they were the flower described by several medieval writers as being put in casks of maturing wine 'to give a pleasant taste and gallant colour.' Chaucer talks of a 'clove gilofre' but there is no evidence that the clove carnation was actually introduced into the UK at that time. It is more likely that what he referred to is the flower bud of *Eugenia aromatica*, which was also used to make a sweet and spicy syrup to pour over pudding.

THE FIRST CORKSCREW

England was the first country to cork wine bottles, much as we do now, using cork imported from Spain and Portugal. Although the date of the invention of the corkscrew is a little hazy, what we do know is that by the eighteenth century people were tired of hacking away at corks with knives and getting bits in their wine, and the search for a machine that would remove a cork perfectly every time was on. It's a search that has perplexed wine lovers ever since!

The first corkscrews took their inspiration from a tool used to get unspent bullets out of rifle barrels, which as you can imagine was a delicate job, and historians believe that adapted versions of these 'gun wormes' were in use by the seventeenth century. The first official corkscrew, however, was designed by Samuel Henshall from Christchurch, Middlesex. On 24 August 1795 he was

granted patent No 2061 for a device we would very much recognise as a corkscrew, which used brute force to pull out the cork once the screw was firmly embedded.

The 'butler's friend' corkscrew which uses leverage to draw a cork smoothly and easily, was patented by German Carl Wienke nearly a century later on 26 May 1882, and is still very popular today.

The other classic corkscrew design, the double wing lever (the sort that you screw in, then carry on screwing to lift the cork out), was patented by Neville Smith Heeley in the UK in 1888 as the A1 Heeley Double Lever, but Americans had to wait another 42 years before they got their own version, when Italian designer Dominick Rosati was granted a US patent and Canadian patent for his version in 1930.

WHAT'S IN A NAME?

The wine industry is takes itself rather seriously, so it's refreshing to know that there are some producers out there with a sense of humour. These are real names.

Ted the Mule (France)
Wild Pig (France)
Fat Bastard (France)
Utter Bastard (France)
Marilyn Merlot (California)
Arrogant Frog Ribet Red (France)
Duck Muck (Australia)
Scraping the Barrel (Spain)
Cardinal Zin (California)
Dog's Bollocks (France)
Ptomaine de Blageurs (California)
Eye of the Toad (California)

ODE TO THE NOBLE GRAPE

Since the 1870s there had existed a small dining club, 'Ye Sette of Odde Volumes' (parodied by Waugh in *Brideshead Revisited*), which had historian André Simon as a member, who attended under the pseudonym 'Vintner'. In November 1931, he read a paper to the Sette, which was afterwards printed in a private edition of 199 copies, under the title *Wine in Shakespeare's Days and Shakespeare's Plays*.

He pointed out that in Shakespeare's day, nobody drank water, as it was not fit to drink. Although the population of Britain was a fraction of what it is today, vastly more wine was imported per head of population and wine was quaffed, not sipped, because of its youth. Beer and real ale were drunk at breakfast and midday and wine in the evening.

No one who was not a vintner was allowed to keep wine in his house but the wine supplied by the taverns was plentiful and cheap, costing 4d a quart.

It was young wine, a year old and freshly broached, shipped in wood and drawn from the wood. Bottles existed then but corks did not until James I's day. Bottles were used to carry the wine to the table but their irregular shape meant that there was no laying down for maturity.

IT'S THE WINE TALKING

Name me any liquid – except our own blood – that flows more intimately and incessantly through the labyrinth of symbols we have conceived to make our status as human beings, from the rudest peasant festival to the mystery of the Eucharist. To take wine into our mouths is to savour a droplet of the river of human history.
Clifton Fadiman, American writer/commentator

GODS OF THE GRAPE

Dionysos was one of the children of Zeus who was raised to godly status (Zeus didn't favour all of his bastard children with immortality). His mother, according to legend, was a Theban woman Semele. Dionysos, usually represented as a good-looking young man, became the god of wine and vegetation, but not just of cheerful intoxication; he also became the god of drunken rage, frenzy, and creativity, acknowledging the link between excess, addiction and creation in the arts. Many experts believe that he was a late introduction to the Olympian pantheon that represented aspects of several nature gods. He was also a god of destruction and death, and of water, and is associated with the fir tree and pine cones, fennel and ivy.

The story of how Dionysos gave man wine is an interesting one and neatly demonstrates how aware the Greeks were of the good and bad aspects of alcohol. Dionysos came to the house of a horticulturist, Ikarios and gave him a vine and instructions on how to rear it and make wine from the juice of its berries. Ikarios followed the god's instructions, made the wine and invited his neighbours over to taste it. They were astonished by its taste and aroma, and began to get merry. Then they drank more and began to fall over. Those not dead drunk thought Ikarios had poisoned them all, beat him to death and threw his body down a well. His daughter, discovering his death, promptly hanged herself.

Female and transvestite worshippers of Dionysos (called Maenads) would periodically leave their ordinary, everyday lives and go into the countryside where they drank and went into a frenzy which was considered god-sent. They would dance and sing to exhaustion and take part in sexual rites – which sounds suspiciously like a good excuse for a knees-up and a break from a mundane life.

CHATEAU CINEMA

Films with wine in the title or as part of the plot

Days of Wine and Roses (1962)
French Kiss (1995)
Blood and Wine (1996)
Last of the Summer Wine (1973)
Spring and Port Wine (1970)
The Six Million Dollar Man: Wine, Women and War (1973, made for TV of course)
Jugular Wine: A Vampire Odyssey (1994)
May Wine (1991)
Almonds and Wine (1999)
Black Wine (2005)
Sideways (2004)
Mondovino (2004)
New Wine (1941)
Strawberries and Wine (2000)
Wine, Woman and Song (many)

WINE AND PHILOSOPHY

'Think of the wonders uncorked by wine' said Horace, and it is very true that philosophers have certainly drunk more than their fair share of wine over the years. Euripedes even wrote a play – *The Bacchae* – about getting drunk on wine. The contemporary philosopher and wine writer Roger Scruton has argued that wine is heightened with meaning and is culturally and morally superior to all other intoxicating agents. Scruton believes that the intoxicating quality of wine is not the same as, for example, poetry – one is a sensual experience, the other is an intellectual experience.

Wine, according to Scruton, is also different to other stimulating or intoxicating substances such as tobacco or hallucinogenic drugs in that the presence of the alcohol remains part of the flavour, like the way an honest person's character is revealed in their face. With strong liquor or marijuana, by contrast, the pleasure of consumption is secondary to the effects, so that for the smoker or alcoholic the urge to get stoned or drunk is more important than the taste of what they are imbibing.

WORDS ON WINE

Hence Burgundy, Claret, and Port,
Away with old Hock and madeira,
Too earthly ye are for my sport;
There's a beverage brighter and clearer.
Instead of a piriful rummer,
My wine overbrims a whole summer;
My bowl is the sky,
And I drink at my eye,
Till I feel in the brain
A Delphian pain –
Then follow, my Caius! then follow:
On the green of the hill
We will drink our fill
Of golden sunshine,
Till our brains intertwine
With the glory and grace of Apollo!
God of the Meridian,
And of the East and West,
To thee my soul is flown,
And my body is earthward press'd.
It is an awful mission,
A terrible division;
And leaves a gulph austere
To be fill'd with worldly fear.
Aye, when the soul is fled
To high above our head,
Affrighted do we gaze
After its airy maze,
As doth a mother wild,
When her young infant child
Is in an eagle's claws –
And is not this the cause
Of madness? – God of Song,
Thou bearest me along
Through sights I scarce can bear:
O let me, let me share
With the hot lyre and thee,
The staid Philosophy.
Temper my lonely hours,
And let me see thy bowers
More unalarm'd!

John Keats,
***Hence Burgundy, Claret
and Port* (1818)**

ALL GREEK TO ME

No vines now exist along the Nile or Tigris and as early as the fifth century BC – Herodotus's day – Egypt was importing wine from Greece. The climate of Egypt did not suit the vine as the Mediterranean did although we know that at some periods vines flourished.

Incidentally, in the early days the Romans imported their wines from Greece and Virgil considered Greek wine superior to Italian: 'Not our Italian wines produce the shape. Or taste or flavour of the Lesbian grape.'

I WISH THEY ALL COULD BE CALIFORNIAN...

- Chardonnay takes up more space than any other wine grape in California, with over 103,000 acres.
- Together, the counties of Napa and Sonoma produce only 9% of all California wine.
- Robert Mondavi built Napa Valley's first new winery after the repeal of Prohibition.
- The wineries of Ernest & Julio Gallo make as much wine in six minutes as does Château Pétrus in one year.
- In the 1906 San Francisco earthquake 30 million gallons of wine were lost.
- The first fine wine grapes in California were planted in downtown Los Angeles at the current site of the Union Train Station where Jean-Louis Vignes (yes, that was his real name), a native of Bordeaux, planted vines in 1833.
- There are over 1,300 'bricks and mortar' wineries in California
- There are about 5,000 Californian grape growers
- Californians produce over 3.12 billion bottles of wine each year
- The total retail value of Californian wine is over $15.2 billion
- California welcomes about 15 million visitors a year (these statistics are pre-*Sideways*)

MY CUP RUNNETH OVER...

Although Champagne wasn't invented until the eighteenth century, urban legend has it that the original saucer-shaped glass was modelled on the breasts of Helen of Troy. Supposedly the Greeks considered drinking wine such a sensual experience that it was deemed appropriate that the most beautiful woman take part in shaping the vessel. Not surprisingly, the French claim this innovation in product design as their own, for centuries later, Diane de Poitiers – Madame de Pompadour (Henri II's mistress) commissioned a court glass-blower to make custom-sized coupes as a gift for Henri, who was a breast-man himself, and had expressed a fantasy of drinking wine from Diane's fair pair. Even later, Marie Antoinette, Queen of France, decided it was time for a re-fit, and had coupes re-shaped in her own image.

Fortunately for the rest of us, she was quite well-endowed.

IT'S THE WINE TALKING

The best use of bad wine is to drive away poor relations.
French proverb

'I cook with wine, sometimes I even add it to the food.'
(WC Fields)

THROUGH A GLASS DARKLY

What is Vin Santo?

a) the Italian patron saint of wine
b) an Italian wine made from dried grapes
c) Italian for so-called noble rot, or botrytis cinerea
d) a spirit made from distilled grape pulp and skins

Answer on page 154.

A BOUQUET OF CRAP

Here's one for advocates of free speech and quality wine. In 2002, French magazine *Lyon Mag* ran an article analysing the reasons that Beaujolais producers were asking for government subsidies to compensate for the 100,000 hectolitres of their unsold wine destined to be turned into vinegar. *Lyon Mag* quoted the head of the Grand Jury of European Tasters as saying that much of Beaujolais wine was 'not proper wine' and that its producers were 'conscious of selling a *vin de merde*' (literally, a s**tty wine). Citing these comments as 'intolerable,' incensed Beaujolais producers sued the magazine for libel. The county court at Villefranche-sur-Saône found in favour of the producers, and ordered *Lyon Mag* to pay €284,143 (a sum that would have forced the magazine to close).

The world's media – even the French press – rallied in support of *Lyon Mag*, one of a small handful of outspoken provincial publications in the country, criticising the court's decision. The fine was lowered to €90,993 in August 2002, but the magazine pursued an appeal. In 2005, the highest court of appeal overturned the decision, saying the defamation case was invalid. The court cited article 10 of the European Convention, indicating that the general public has the right to hear variety of opinions on any subject. The ruling stated that 'The publication of criticism, even severe criticism, concerning wine cannot constitute a crime in the context of a public debate on state subsidies given to winemakers and investigations into the causes of over-production and falling consumption.' This is all a bit ironic, as 'barnyardy' is a term that has long been applied to wines with an earthy, farm animal characteristic. Tasters can voice their opinion freely without fear of putting their foot in it.

TOASTS WITH THE MOST

It gives me great pleasure.
George Bernard Shaw – this quote takes on a whole new
meaning when you know that the dinner topic was sex

May you live all the years of your life.
Jonathan Swift

May the people who dance on your grave get cramps in their legs.
From *The Joys of Yiddish*

To temperance… in moderation.
Lem Motlow

Here's looking at you, kid.'
Humphrey Bogart, to Ingrid Bergman, in *Casablanca* (1942)

*I drink to your charm, your beauty and your brains – which gives
you a rough idea of how hard up I am for a drink.*
Groucho Marx

May bad fortune follow you all your days and never catch up with you.
Anon

*As best man at a wedding dinner, I reminded the groom of the advice I had given
him which he chose not to follow and which led him to be in the wedding.*
Brent H Curtis

And here's to you, Mrs Robinson.
Simon and Garfunkel

ALL GREEK TO ME

Never ones to miss a commercial trick, the Ancient Greeks advertised their main three exportable commodities on their coinage – coins featuring corn, oil and wine have been dug up by archaeologists. The modern ad men are clearly missing a trick by not getting Coke or Nike on the back of the 50 pence piece.

IT'S THE WINE TALKING

I drink Champagne when I'm happy and when I'm sad. Sometimes I drink it when I'm alone. When I have company, I consider it obligatory. I trifle with it if I'm not hungry and drink it when I am. Otherwise I never touch it…unless I'm thirsty.
Lily Bollinger, née Elizabeth Law, who married into the Bollinger family and took over the business upon her husband Jacques' death in 1941

WORDS ON WINE

'Now, J – for a glass of Champagne – take it out of the pail – nay, man! not with both hands round the middle, unless you like it warm – by the neck, so,' showing him how to do it and pouring him a glass of still Champagne. 'This won't do,' said Jorrocks, holding it up to the candle; 'garsoon! garsoon! – no good – no bon – no fizzay, no fizzay,' giving the bottom of the bottle a slap with his hand to rouse it. 'Oh, but this is still Champagne,' explained the Yorkshireman, 'and far the best.' 'I don't think so,' retorted Mr. Jorrocks, emptying the glass into his water-stand. 'Well, then, have a bottle of the other,' rejoined the Yorkshireman, ordering one. 'And who's to pay for it?' inquired Mr. Jorrocks. 'Oh, never mind that – care killed the cat – give a loose to pleasure for once, for it's a poor heart that never rejoices. Here it comes, and "may you never know what it is to want," as the beggar boys say. Now, let's see you treat it like a philosopher – the wire is off, so you've nothing to do but cut the string,

and press the cork on one side with your thumb. Nay! you've cut both sides!' Fizz, pop, bang, and away went the cork close past the ear of an old deaf general, and bounded against the wall. 'Come, there's no mischief done, so pour out the wine. Your good health, old boy, may you live for a thousand years, and I be there to count them! – Now, that's what I call good,' observed the Yorkshireman, holding up his glass, 'see how it dulls the glass, even to the rim – Champagne isn't worth a copper unless it's iced – is it, Colonel?' 'Vy, I don't know – carn't say I like it so werry cold; it makes my teeth chatter, and cools my courage as it gets below – Champagne certainly gives one werry gentlemanly ideas, but for a continuance, I don't know but I should prefer mild hale.' 'You're right, old boy, it does give one very gentlemanly ideas, so take another glass, and you'll fancy yourself an emperor. – Your good health again.'

Robert Smith Surtees,
***Jorrock's Jaunts and Jollities* (1838)**

IMPORTANT WINE RIVERS

Gironde (the main river of Bordeaux, France)

Garonne (feeds the Gironde)

Dordogne (feeds the Gironde)

Loire (the longest river in France, and said to be
the last 'wild river' in Western Europe)

Rhône (the fastest and most powerful river in France)

Rhine (the longest river in Germany)

Moselle, **Saar** and **Ruwer** (Germany, together they make up a magic three)

Ebro (Spain, thought to be the root of the word Iberia)

Douro/Duero (one of the major rivers of Portugal
and Spain, with its outlet at Oporto)

Murray (Australia's second-longest river – the longest is its tributary, the **Darling** –
forms the border between Victoria and New South Wales)

Margaret (town and river of the same name in Western Australia)

Danube (Europe's second-longest river, it flows through 10 countries)

A LOAD OF OLD BULL

In 1308, Clement V, the former archbishop of Bordeaux, moved the site of the papacy to Avignon and the papal court quickly developed a taste for the quantities of Beaune that were dispatched there. By 1364 they were hooked. In a trade embargo of bathetic proportions, the Avignon Pope Urban V issued a papal bull to the Abbot of Cîteaux, forbidding him to send any more of his wine to Rome upon pain of excommunication.

Clearly, threatening a supplier with his mortal soul in order to ensure a regular supply had a profound effect. Beaune became not just the papal exile's drink of choice but almost the 'fifth element' according to the scholar Petrarch. In 1366, Petrarch begged Urban V to return the seat of the papacy to Rome, adding that otherwise he might face resistance from the cardinals because there was no Beaune in Italy and they did not believe that they could live a happy life without it.

WINE WORDS

Toast

The usage as a wish of good health may have started in ancient Rome, where a piece of spiced, burned bread was supposedly dropped into wine to improve its flavour and to help absorb the sediment. (The English also lay claim to this tradition.) Later on, in the eighteenth century when communal baths were popular, legend has it that someone drank a cup of bath-water to the health of a lady and a nearby jokester quipped, 'I do not like the liquor so much, but I should love to have the toast' (referring to the lady). Eventually, drinking to someone's health became known as drinking a toast. One explanation for the tradition of clinking glasses seems to point to a gesture wherein each person spills a bit of wine into the other's glass for assurance that nobody (or everybody) is poisoned. Another rationale is that in the Middle Ages, alcohol was thought to contain actual 'spirits' (eg demons, as in the 'demon rum'). The chiming of bells and other sounds were thought to drive spirits away, hence the clinking of glasses rendering the contents safe to drink.

A FINGER OF GOLD, PLEASE

Ever wondered what Peter the Great of Russia and Frederick I of Prussia drank? The answer is inevitably Tokay, the most famous wine in the eighteenth century that was reputed to contain gold. In fact, Tokay was the emperor's new clothes of wine, being no more than the product of a fashionable whim for its peculiar flavour. This whimsy was first circulated by the Italian humanist Marzio Galeotto at the beginning of the sixteenth century who, following a visit to Hungary claimed that there were golden shoots on some vines in Tokay.

The theory was even tested out by the physician and alchemist Paracelsus of Basel, who performed minute experiments on the grapes and wines to no avail. However, fully aware of the value of the trade, he came up with an obscure and somewhat craven statement, designed to serve all parties and keep the sales of Tokay strong: 'The vine of the Hegyalja region is the most magnificent plant because in that country vegetals are allied to minerals, and sunshine, like a thread of gold, passes through stocks and roots into the rock.'

Yeah, right.

IT'S THE WINE TALKING

I love Champagne because it always tastes as though my foot's asleep.
Art Buchwald, American humourist

ALL GREEK TO ME

Most of what we know about Roman and Greek cookery comes from *De Re Coquinaria* (or 'On Cooking') by Apicius, who recorded the richness and complexity of fine dining during the reigns of the Caesars. No one really knows who Apicius was – there are three noted gourmets of that name recorded during that period – but 'his' writing preserves what was being eaten at banquets and in the houses of the rich all across Roman Europe, with its access to China and the Indies for spices. The Roman's didn't distil liquor and didn't brew beer, so wine was their staple for drinking and for cooking. It turns up in almost every dish, including *liquamen* or *garum*, a sauce very similar to Vietnamese nam pla, made from rotted mackerel entrails with salt, vinegar, parsley, wine and herbs, which was the Roman's favourite condiment.

Meals often began with spiced wine to accompany the *gustatio* (hors d'oeuvres). To make *Conium Paradoxes*, or Extraordinary Spiced Wine, he advises:

'Put fifteen pounds of honey into a bronze vessel, having previously poured in two pints of wine. In this way, the wine shall be boiled off in the melting honey. The mixture is heated by a slow fire of dry wood and stirred, while boiling, with a wooden rod. If it begins to boil over, pour more wine over it. After the fire has been withdrawn, the remaining mixture will settle. When it has grown cold, another fire is kindled beneath. This second fire is followed by a third and only then can the mixture be moved away from the hearth. On the following day it is skimmed. Then add four ounces of ground pepper, three scruples of mastic [a gum that is tapped from the mastic tree, just as maple syrup is, which gives a resinous flavour], a single handful each of saffron leaves and spikenard [an Indian tree with fragrant leaves, used in Roman cooking much as we use bay leaves], and five dried date stones, the dates having previously been softened in wine of the right quantity and quality to produce a soft mixture. When all this has been done pour eighteen pints of mild wine into the vessel. Hot coals are added to the finished product.'

'Gosh, this cork's a devil to remove'.

SINGERS WITH WINE ON THEIR MIND

Lilac Wine (Jeff Buckley, 1994)
Lips of Wine (Andy Williams, 1957)
Hey Brother, Pour the Wine (Dean Martin, 1964)
Little Ole Wine Drinker Me (Dean Martin, 1967)
Me and My Wine (Def Leppard, 1980)
Spill the Wine (War, 1970)
Strawberry Wine (Deana Carter,1995, and also the Dixie Chicks)
Sweet Wine (Cream, 1970)
Wine Colored Roses (George Jones, 1986)
Wine into Water (T Graham Brown, 1998)
Wine, Women an' Song (Whitesnake, 1981)
Wine, Women and Song (Loretta Lynn, 1964)
Summer Wine (Nancy Sinatra, 1968)

KEEPING STUART SPIRITS UP

While Elizabeth I took a patrician view of taxes on wine, arguing that bread and drink were necessary to existence and should have their price fixed by law, James I, who inherited the English throne in 1603, created an open market in wine. This false act of generosity ensured that he could take his cut from the many wine licences he granted to speculators who could afford them, including the royal privileges of prisage and butlerage.

Men bought from the King for a lump sum rights to sell wine on to the public at whatever rate they chose. There was no excise duty on wine until 1643, during the Civil War, but licensees were able to control the price of wine among themselves and prices rose steeply. This price rise led to tavern keepers looking for other alcoholic beverages to offer their customers that represented better value for money.

Within a few years, as the impositions bit, many people turned to brewing their own at home. There are a few Shakespearian references to 'strong waters'. In *Twelfth Night* they are called 'a midwife's tipple', and in *Romeo and Juliet* the nurse asks for them. Such spirits were usually made from wine dregs and sour ale, and were sold in the street by 'brandy women'.

THROUGH A GLASS DARKLY

Two winemakers stand over an open barrel of red wine. One says 'I bet this barrel is more than half full'. Her colleague says, 'No it's not – it's less than half full'. Without removing any wine from the barrel or using tools to measure the contents, how can they figure out who is right?

Answer on page 154.

Answer on page 154.

GREAT WINE RECIPES

Dolmades

Well, it doesn't do to forget the vine leaves! Dolmades are made all around the Eastern Mediterranean. In Turkish they're just a 'dolma', in Armenia a 'tolma'. In Romania they become 'sarma' ('sarmale' in the plural). The basic format is savoury rice wrapped in vine leaves, with or without meat. Some countries add raisins and pine nuts, others chopped mint and parsley.

Finely chop half a large onion and fry in olive oil until beginning to brown. If using meat, add about four ounces of lean minced beef to the pan, break up and fry until brown. Add half a teaspoon lemon zest and two ounces of pine nuts, and stir. Season with a pinch of cinnamon, salt and black pepper, then stir in two ounces of uncooked long grain rice. Stir again to coat the grains of rice in oil.

Pour in quarter of a pint of chicken stock, put on a lid and reduce the heat to low. Leave the rice to steam for 10 minutes then stir in two tablespoons of chopped flat leaf parsley and one tablespoon of dill or mint.

When the mixture is cool take some vacuum-packed vine leaves and drop into boiling water for five minutes to soften and clean. Place a dried leaf vein side up and put a spoonful of savoury rice just above the stem. Fold the stem end over the filling, fold in the sides, and then roll up quite loosely – the rice is only part cooked and will expand. When you've used up all your leaves or all your rice take a large frying pan and if you have spare or split leaves, use these to line the bottom of the pan. Lay your parcels in a single layer, and pour over a pint of chicken stock mixed with one tablespoon of lemon juice and two of olive oil.

Cover and simmer gently for about one and half hours, without removing the lid. When the liquid has evaporated they're done.

GODS OF THE GRAPE

Jesus's first miracle, though rather less spectacular than making the lame walk and the blind see, is a party trick of the first order. It describes how, at a wedding in Cana, in Galilee, Jesus turned water into wine when the host ran out of drink. The Virgin Mary was among the guests, and when Jesus and his apostles arrived they asked for some wine, and Mary told them it had run out, at which point Jesus uttered the rather perplexing 'Woman, what have I to do with thee? Mine hour is not yet come' and then proceeded to sort out the catering problem.

First he got the servants to fill six water pots to the brim with water and then told them to draw off water as thought it was wine. When the water was served to the feasters, it tasted like wine. 'This beginning of miracles did Jesus in Cana of Galilee, and manifested forth his glory; and his disciples believed in him.'

SOZZLED SIMPSONS

Beer is generally the beverage of choice in the Simpson household. That is, until Bart flushes a cherry bomb down the school toilet in the infamous episode 'The Crepes of Wrath'. As punishment Bart is sent to France via a student exchange and ends up working for some crooks whose aim is to put antifreeze in their wine.

Meanwhile, the luckless Simpsons receive in return Adil Hoxha, an Albanian exchange student-cum-spy.

Some typical Simpsons style wine-related banter follows:

Bart: So basically I met one nice French person.
Lisa: It's good to see you!

Bart reflects on the sentiment while Marge asks to try the wine Bart brought as Homer struggles to open it.

Homer: Some wise-guy stuck a cork in the bottle!
Bart: Mon pere! Quel bouffon!
Homer: Ya here that, Marge? My boy speaks French!

Homer finally uncorks the bottle with his teeth.

WORDS ON WINE

Go fetch to me a pint o' wine,
An' fill it in a silver tassie;
That I may drink before I go
A service to my bonnie lassie.
The boat rocks at the pier o' Leith,
Fu' loud the wind blaws frae the Ferry,
The ship rides by the Berwick-law,
And I maun leave my bonnie Mary.

The trumpets sound, the banners fly,
The glittering spears are rankèd ready;
The shouts o' war are heard afar,
The battle closes thick and bloody;
But it's not the roar o' sea or shore
Wad mak me langer wish to tarry;
Nor shouts o' war that's heard afar
It's leaving thee, my bonnie Mary.

Robert Burns, *A Farewell* (1786)

A PEARL BEFORE AN (UNDOUBTED) SWINE

According to Pliny the Elder, Cleopatra once drank a pearl earring dissolved in wine vinegar after wagering Marc Antony that she could serve him the most expensive meal ever prepared. He accepted her bet then refused her offer of the other earring and, of course, lost the bet. The value of the imbibed pearl was reputed to be 30 tonnes of gold.

A pearl will dissolve in vinegar, because calcium carbonate neutralises the acetic acid in vinegar, but only if ground into a powder first. Such dissolved pearls were used in medieval and Renaissance Europe and are also prescribed in Asian medicine.

Being mostly calcium, pearls can't hurt you and might even help; a recent study of a medicinal mixture with calcium from the Akoya pearl oyster showed that it reduced the cholesterol level in rats.

THROUGH A GLASS DARKLY

What is Crémant?
a) a town in Burgundy
b) a kind of Sherry
c) a sparkling wine
d) a type of soft soil
Answer on page 154.

DECANTER BANTER

How to get a grotty decanter clean.
If you can't get at all of the insides, half fill it with warm water and some washing up liquid. Pour in about two tablespoons of uncooked rice and swirl it around. Over 30 minutes keep going back and giving it a little swirl. By the end any stains on the base should have some off. Rinse out and leave to dry upside down.

Meanwhile, to get out a decanter stopper that's stuck, wrap the decanter itself in a hot, wet towel to expand the glass, and gently tap the stopper on opposite sides with a wooden spoon handle. If that fails, get hold of an eye dropper or similar and drizzle a few drops of oil around the lip. Leave in a warm place – like an airing cupboard – and in a few hours the stopper should be free again.

WHEN MARTINIS JUST AREN'T DE RIGUEUR

Bond's wines: Mouton Rothschild
While having dinner with Goldfinger in the eponymous 1964 film, Sean Connery sips Mouton Rothschild 1947, while George Lazenby consumes half a bottle in *On Her Majesty's Secret Service* (1969). In *Diamonds are Forever* (1971), Connery spots Wint the villain, who, when pretending to be a wine steward, opens a bottle of Mouton '55 without realising it's a claret. When Moore and M dine together in *Moonraker* (1979), M, far from a cheap date, orders a Mouton Rothschild '34.

IT'S THE WINE TALKING

*My dear girl, there are some things that just aren't done, such as
drinking Dom Pérignon '53 above the temperature of 38° Fahrenheit.
That's just as bad as listening to the Beatles without ear-muffs!*
James Bond, in *Goldfinger* (1964). (As a cinematic aside,
Dom Pérignon 1953 was also Marilyn Monroe's favourite fizz.)

TOPPING BEVERAGES

If you want to kill somebody by poisoning their wine, try Aconite. Aconite, variously referred to as wolf's bane, devil's helmet and blue rocket, was hailed by the Greeks as the Queen of Poisons, created from the saliva of Cerberus. In fact, it wasn't. It comes from the garden plant monkshood (*Aconitum anglicum*) whose leaves and roots yield the potent ingredient, aconitine.

The powder is easily dissolvable and white, with only one fiftieth of a grain proving deadly to the cardio-vascular system, central nervous system and gastro-intestinal tract.

If the dose is large enough, it produces a severe burning sensation from the throat to the abdomen, with a tingling feeling soon spreading to the hands and feet. The victim will be clear-headed until death comes, usually from failure of the respiratory system – between eight minutes and four hours after the poison is administered.

An alternative is arsenic, which could be bought by the pound until the 1851 Arsenic Act forbade the sale of arsenic compounds unless the purchaser was known to the pharmacist. Moreover, manufacturers were required to mix each pound of arsenic with one ounce of soot or indigo colouring, making it difficult for poisoners to slip arsenic in to food and beverages.

We are exposed to about 8mg of arsenic a day, but 42mg would kill a 70kg adult. The symptoms are an irritation and burning sensation in the throat, faintness, nausea and depression accompanied by weakness and abdominal pain, which feels as though red hot coals have been applied to the stomach, throat constriction and a furring of the tongue.

Within 12 to 18 hours the symptoms progress to violent diarrhoea, accompanied by painful cramps in the calves and bowels, all while still conscious, finally followed by death.

WORDS ON WINE

Day and night my thoughts incline
To the blandishments of wine:
Jars were made to drain, I think,
Wine, I know, was made to drink.

When I die, (the day be far!)
Should the potters make a jar
Out of this poor clay of mine,
Let the jar be filled with wine!

**Richard Henry Stoddard,
'The Jar' from *Oriental Songs***

WHAT WILL THEY THINK OF NEXT?

Here are some of the inventions and innovations that clever wine industry folks are working on these days. Genius or gimmick? You be the judge.

- Glow-in-the-dark wine labels: Carneros della Notte (Carneros of the Night) may be the first producer to stick luminous labels on its bottles, part of its strategy to highlight Pinot Noir... geddit?

- Temperature sensitive labels. Several brands are now affixing labels using thermo-sensitive ink to let eager drinkers know when their white, rosé and sparkling wines are ready to drink (generally between 11°C and 13°C)

- Talking wine labels. An Italian label maker has developed a micro-chipped label onto which a voice can be recorded – for example, the winemaker expounding on the virtues of the vintage.

- A remedy for cork taint. This really is the holy grail, for while most of the unpleasant aromas detected in wine these days have nothing to do with real cork taint (a bacteria that affects cork), wines bottled before the cork industry developed measures to prevent cork taint are susceptible. There can be nothing more disappointing than opening an old bottle only to find it undrinkable, and 'Dream Taste' – a product made from an ionised material called a copolymer – is meant to absorb the cork taint molecule and render the wine palatable in an hour.

- But are they dishwasher safe? Breathable crystal wine glasses, made by Eisch, have undergone a special treatment that allows them to aerate wine in two to four minutes. Breathe deeply but don't inhale...

WHAT'S IN A NAME?

Here are some more wines with a sense of humour. They're all real names.

Goats do Roam (South Africa – a spoof of Côtes du Rhône)
Cat's Pee on a Gooseberry Bush (New Zealand)
Vampire's Reserve (Romania)
Chardonn Alien (California – where else?)
The Unpronounceable Grape (Hungary – it's actually 'Cserszegi Fıszeres')
Marge 'n' Tina (Californian homage to Argentinian varietals)
Cochon Mignon (France – means cute pig)
Red Bicyclette (France)
Mélange de Trois (California)
Truth Serum (Australia)
Working Girl White (Washington)
Go Girl Red (Washington)
Rosé the Riveter (Washington)

NYEAH, NYEAH, SO THERE...

In February 2005, Her Majesty the Queen showed her support for London's 2012 Olympic bid by banning French wines from a royal banquet served to the International Olympic Committee. Rather than serving Champagne, for example, she offered an English sparkling wine – along with various wines from Australia and New Zealand. In addition, the menu card – usually written in French – was presented in English.

Several months later, French President Jacques Chirac showed characteristic diplomacy when he insulted not one, but two countries – denouncing British cuisine as 'the worst in Europe after Finland. It's the country with the worst food.' He reportedly went further, joking with other political leaders that former NATO Secretary General George Robertson, a Scot, had made him try an unappetising Scottish dish (most likely haggis) and saying 'that's where our problems with NATO come from'.

It goes without saying that these two items are not related. London, of course, subsequently won the Olympic bid.

IT'S THE WINE TALKING

Wine snob – a man or woman who drinks the label and the price.
Olof Wijk, UK wine merchant and pundit

WORDS ON WINE

Placed between a young lady just out and a dowager of grimly Gorgonesque aspect, you hesitate how to open a conversation. Your first attempts are singularly ineffectual, only eliciting a dropping fire of monosyllables. You envy the placidly languid young gentleman opposite, limp as his fast-fading camellia, and seated next to Belle Breloques, who is certain, in racing parlance, to make the running for him. But even that damsel seems preoccupied with her fan and despite her aplomb, hesitates to break the icy silence. The two City friends of the host are lost in mute speculation as to the future price of indigo or Ionian Bank shares, while their wives seem to be mentally summarising the exact cost of each others' toilettes. Their daughters, or somebody else's daughters, are desperately jerking out monosyllabic responses to feeble remarks concerning the weather, the theatres, operatic debutantes, the people in the Row, aestheticism, and kindred topics from a couple of F.O. men. Little Snapshot, the wit, on the other side of the Gorgon, has tried to lead up to a story but has found himself as it were frozen in the bud. When lo! The butler softly sibillates in your ear the magic word 'Champagne,' and as it flows, creaming and frothing, into your glass, a change comes over the spirit of your vision.

The hostess brightens, the host coruscates. The young lady on your right suddenly develops into a charming girl, with becoming appreciation of your pet topics and an astounding aptness for repartee. The Gorgon thaws, and implores Mr Snapshot, whose jests are popping as briskly as the corks, not to be so dreadfully funny, or he will positively kill her. Belle Breloques can always talk, and now her tongue rattles faster than ever, till the languid one arouses himself like a giant refreshed, and gives her as good as he gets. The City men expatiate in cabbalistic language on the merits of some mysterious speculation, the prospective returns from which increase with each fresh bottle. One of their wives is discussing church decoration with a hitherto silent curate, and the other is jabbering botany to a red faced warrior. The juniors are in full swing, and ripples of silvery laughter rise in accompaniment to the beaded bubbles all around the table.

Henry Vizetelly, *A History of Champagne* (1882)

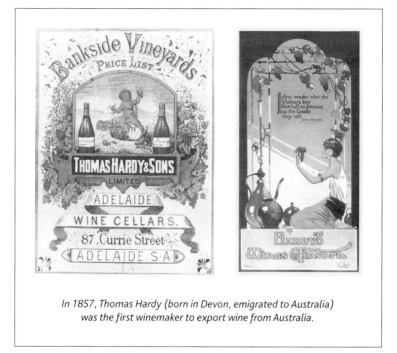

In 1857, Thomas Hardy (born in Devon, emigrated to Australia) was the first winemaker to export wine from Australia.

GODS OF THE GRAPE

The Sumerians, like the Ancient Egyptians, were heavily into wine, and had several goddesses associated with grapes and wine drinking. Geshtin (also known as Geshtinanna and Gestinanna) was the Sumerian goddess of the vine and vineyards. Her name means literally 'Lady of the Vine'. The Sumerians also borrowed Spenta Armaiti, the Persian goddess of vineyards – they were obviously anxious their vineyards got a lot of protection. As well as the vineyard itself there was also Ninkasi, the 'Lady Who Fills The Mouth', the goddess of intoxicating drink.

IT'S THE WINE TALKING

What is man, when you come to think upon him, but a minutely set, ingenious machine for turning, with infinite artfulness, the red wine of Shiraz into urine?
Karen Blixen (aka Isak Dinesen), Danish writer

RED, WHITE AND THE BLUES

Think you know your red from your white? Think again. Several studies have proved that wine drinkers – even experts – cannot tell the difference based on aroma and flavour. One ground-breaking experiment by the Bordeaux-based researcher Frédéric Brochet even went so far as to demonstrate that the more expertise someone has, the more cultural context clouds his/her judgement. Brochet conducted two studies.

In one, 54 high profile wine experts from Bordeaux tasted several different bottles – including a white wine which had been coloured red by the addition of a flavourless substance. Nobody spotted this, leading Brochet to conclude that the expectation that the wine was red influenced the tasters' perception. In the second experiment, 57 experts tried the same bottle of average quality Bordeaux, twice. On the first try, the wine was labelled as a high quality grand cru, while the second time, it was labelled as a cheap table wine. When the experts were under the impression that the wine

was a grand cru, they described it as agreeable, complex and balanced – all qualities associated with such a wine. When they thought it was table wine, they described it as weak, light, flat, sharp and even faulty. Forty tasters thought the wine was good quality when they believed it was expensive, but only 12 thought so when it was cheap. Brochet, who has studied the brain activity of wine tasters, has found that the parts of the brain that process information about colour and knowledge work alongside those that process flavour and smell. So what we perceive is an amalgam of vision, taste and thought. Likewise, he pointed out that the molecule that gives red wine its taste of red fruits (currants and raspberries, for example) is the same as that which gives white wine the taste of stone fruits like apricot or peach. You can try this at home: Riedel and others make black tasting glasses which make it impossible to see the colour of the wine in the glass, and you can blindfold yourself so as not to see the wine if it drips as you sip it.

SIZE MATTERS

While glass bottles have been used since the seventeenth century, it was only with moulded bottles that capacity could be standardised, and imperial volumes were only converted to metric in the 1980s, to conform to the 'Système International d'Unités'.

The 75 ml bottle is now bar far the most common, but hey – there are times when 75 ml just isn't enough (or when it's too much). For those occasions, there are:

Half bottle 37.5ml
Bottle 750ml
Magnum .... 2 bottles
Marie-Jeanne .... 3 bottles
Double Magnum .... 4 bottles
Jeroboam .... 4 bottles *(Champagne or Burgundy)*, 6 bottles *(Bordeaux)*
Rehoboam .... 6 bottles *(Champagne)*
Imperial .... 8 bottles *(Bordeaux)*
Methuselah .... 8 bottles *(Champagne or Burgundy)*
Salmanazar .... 12 bottles *(Champagne)*
Balthazar .... 16 bottles *(Champagne)*

and the king of them all...

Nebuchadnezzar .... 20 bottles *(Champagne)*

GODS OF THE GRAPE

Mabon is the Wiccan or Neo Pagan harvest festival which is particularly associated with wine and wine deities. Because Wicca is pantheistic its rituals bring in elements of all sorts of other religions and call upon a wide range of gods. Wicca celebrates eight solar holidays or sabbats, with Mabon, falling around 21 September in the northern hemisphere. Mabon celebrates the fruitfulness of the earth and emphasises sharing its blessing. Also called Harvest Home, this holiday is a ritual of thanksgiving for the fruits of the earth and a recognition of the need to share them in order to secure the ongoing favour of the Goddess who is central to Wiccan worship. However it's not an authentic pagan festival as the autumn equinox was not celebrated in Celtic countries.

WORDS ON WINE

In spite of the melancholy which was consuming me, we were preparing to welcome the New Year in with exceptional festiveness, and awaited midnight with some impatience. The fact is, we had in reserve two bottles of Champagne, the real thing, with the label of Veuve Clicquot; this treasure I had won the previous autumn in a bet with the station-master of D. when I was drinking with him at a christening. It sometimes happens during a lesson in mathematics, when the very air is still with boredom, a butterfly flutters into the class-room; the boys toss their heads and begin watching its flight with interest, as though they saw before them not a butterfly but something new and strange; in the same way ordinary Champagne, chancing to come into our dreary station, roused us. We sat in silence looking alternately at the clock and at the bottles.

When the hands pointed to five minutes to twelve I slowly began uncorking a bottle. I don't know whether I was affected by the vodka, or whether the bottle was wet, but all I remember is that when the cork flew up to the ceiling with a bang, the bottle slipped from my hands and hit the floor. Not more than a glass of the wine was spilt, as I managed to catch the bottle and put my thumb over the foaming neck.

'Well, may the New Year bring you happiness!' I said, filling two glasses. 'Drink!'

My wife took her glass and fixed her frightened eyes on me. Her face was pale and wore a look of horror.

'Did you drop the bottle?' she asked.

'Yes. But what of that?'

'It's unlucky,' she said, putting down her glass and turning paler still. 'It's a bad omen. It means that some misfortune will happen to us this year.'

'What a silly thing you are,' I sighed. 'You are a clever woman, and yet you talk as much nonsense as an old nurse. Drink.'

'God grant it is nonsense, but... something is sure to happen! You'll see.'

She did not even sip her glass, she moved away and sank into thought. I uttered a few stale commonplaces about superstition, drank half a bottle, paced up and down, and then went out of the room.

Outside there was the still frosty night in all its cold, inhospitable beauty. The moon and two fluffy clouds beside it hung just over the station, motionless as though glued to the spot, and looked as though waiting for something. A faint transparent light came from them and touched the white earth softly, as though afraid of wounding her modesty, and lighted up everything – the snowdrifts, the embankment... It was still.

Anton Chekhov, *Champagne* (1887)

'What a fiasco!'

FOR HEAVEN'S SAKE

December is the *bounenkai* or 'forget the year' party season in Japan and Japanese sake (*nihonshu*) is, after beer, the drink of choice for obliteration at this time. Sake is an important part of Shinto religion and Japanese culture. It is a clear liquid, with around a 15% alcohol content, which is brewed from rice and spring water. After the rice is washed, soaked, steamed and cooled, fermentation starts by adding *koji* rice. Sake can be served hot (*atsukan*) or cold (*hiyazake*) from a ceramic flask called a *tokkuri*. It is then poured into a small cup called an *ochoko* before drinking.

A couple of sake rituals are worth noting before drinking in Japan. Firstly, do not forget to say '*Kampai*' or cheers before you begin drinking, and it is polite to pour sake into each other's cups when you are drinking in company.

FOR MEDICINAL PURPOSES ONLY

In the Middle Ages it was common-place to drink too much at feasts, especially during the grand feasting period from Christmas until Twelfth Night. Lent was also notorious for heavy drinking (possibly because of the boring and salty diet imposed even on courtiers; salt fish went down more easily with a flagon or two of wine! So it's not a surprise that medieval medicine is full of cures for the 'Migrane' and 'For A Man That Is Sick In His Stomach'.

For headaches apply a poultice of hot barley and herbs, including betony, a popular herb at the time which contains betonicine, stachydrine and trigonelline, still used to treat migraine today. Vervain, which can be found in modern nerve tonics, was also used. Lying down quietly while the poultice was wrapped around your head can't have hurt either.

For wind, a powder made from cumin and anise, steeped in wine and then dried and ground up, was recommended. Much of medieval medicine is concerned with digestive disorders, probably as a result of a diet high in pulses but with very few fresh vegetables or fruits. When sick to your stomach after over-indulging, the remedy was to boil a pound of cumin in stale ale and drink the resulting liquid lukewarm, while the boiled cumin dregs were put in a linen bag and laid on the stomach to warm it up. As recently as the 1930s some people still used cumin poultices for stomach cramps. Stale ale, in this case, doesn't mean something nasty, it simply means beer that's been kept for a certain amount of time to allow it to mature.

IT'S THE WINE TALKING

Wine comes in at the mouth
And love comes in at the eye;
That's all we shall know for truth
Before we grow old and die.

WB Yeats, from *The Green Helmet and Other Poems* (1910) –
and also on the wall of one of the world's greatest wine bars, Ely's in Dublin

THROUGH A GLASS DARKLY

Wine snobs may get their corkscrews in a twist about the prevalence of somewhat interchangeable, easy-to-drink brands – but they certainly go down well with many consumers. See if you can recognise these.

a) MOB SLOSH ILL – hint: sponsors of hit TV comedy *Will & Grace*
b) ACRE BE JOCKS – hint: sponsors of hit TV show *Friends*
c) WALLET OILY – hint: the most-imported wine in the US
d) ISLAND MEN – hint: these wines often come in bins

Answer on page 154.

PULLING THE PLUG

French wine growers are increasingly being priced out of a very competitive market, as an average hectare of French vineyard produces less than two fifths of a hectare in the young pretenders, Chile and Argentina. As recently as the 1990s, one in every three imported bottles bought by the American was French. Today, it is down to just 15%.

Added to this, the average French person now drinks only half as much as in the 1960s, which is creating a great deal of surplus product. Enter the EU, which has been asked to provide around €300m to subsidise the industrial distillation of one billion litres of wine of which 25% will be French. This proposal is seen as a way of dealing with an ever-deepening wine lake and as a fresh start for the struggling wine industry.

The big shock is how much of this is quality Apellation d'Origine Controlée and not the lesser Vin de Pays. Under the proposals, some 200 million litres of AOC wine and 50 million litres of Vin de Pays would be distilled for industrial purposes, mainly for fuel and the pharmaceutical industry.

For the first time in 10 years, France alone has 200 million litres of surplus of wine as a result of the abundant 2004 vintage, with an estimated and heartbreaking 100 million litres of this coming from Bordeaux alone.

GODS OF THE GRAPE

Amethyst comes from the Greek *amethustos* (the Greeks believed that anyone wearing an amethyst could not get drunk). This idea came from the legend that Bacchus, the Roman god of wine, created this lovely purple stone from a beautiful maiden called Amethyst. Following an insult, Bacchus had worked himself up into a rage and vowed to have a tiger devour the next person that he met (as you do). But he was foiled when the girl selected called on the goddess Diana to save her.

Diana turned the girl into a beautiful white crystal. Filled with remorse, Bacchus poured wine over the stone maiden, turning her violet and this was the origin of the legend.

WORDS ON WINE

Though I, alas! a pris'ner be,
My trade is prisoners to set free.
No slave his lord's commands obeys
With such insinuating ways.
My genius piercing, sharp, and bright,
Wherein the men of wit delight.
The clergy keep me for their ease,
And turn and wind me as they please.
A new and wondrous art I show
Of raising spirits from below;
In scarlet some, and some in white;
They rise, walk round, yet never fright
In at each mouth the spirits pass,
Distinctly seen as through a glass.
O'er head and body make a rout,
And drive at last all secrets out;
And still, the more I show my art,
The more they open every heart.
A greater chemist none than I
Who, from materials hard and dry,

Have taught men to extract with skill
More precious juice than from a still.
Although I'm often out of case,
I'm not ashamed to show my face.
Though at the tables of the great
I near the sideboard take my seat;
Yet the plain 'squire, when dinner's done,
Is never pleased till I make one;
He kindly bids me near him stand,
And often takes me by the hand.
I twice a-day a-hunting go,
And never fail to seize my foe;
And when I have him by the poll,
I drag him upward from his hole;
Though some are of so stubborn kind,
I'm forced to leave a limb behind.
I hourly wait some fatal end;
For I can break, but scorn to bend.

Jonathan Swift et al,
On a Corkscrew **(c.1724)**

CHAMPAGNE CHARLIES

Champagne and orange juice is a great drink. The orange improves the Champagne. The Champagne definitely improves the orange.
Philip, Duke of Edinburgh

Some people wanted Champagne and caviar when they should have had beer and hot dogs.
President Dwight D Eisenhower

My only regret in life is that I did not drink more Champagne.
John Maynard Keynes

A single glass of Champagne imparts a feeling of exhilaration. The nerves are braced, the imagination is agreeably stirred; the wits become more nimble. A bottle produces the contrary effect. Excess causes a comatose insensibility. So it is with war: and the quality of both is best discovered by sipping.
Winston Churchill

Champagne does have one regular drawback: swilled as a regular thing a certain sourness settles in the tummy, and the result is permanent bad breath. Really incurable.
Truman Capote

ALL GREEK TO ME

It has always puzzled archaeologists that the Greeks, who were such a practical people, should have lighted upon a shape like that of an amphora for their main storage vessel. Why not have something that stood upright on its own? One explanation suggested is that the sediment in the wine stayed in the body of the amphora and sunk to the bottom and the clear wine rose up the neck to be ladled out.

It has also been suggested, more plausibly, that the amphorae were slung from the beams in workshops and tipped up to disgorge their contents.

In the end, the explanation might be quite simple: that the Greeks admired the curvy and feminine proportions of the amphora and for them, beauty was more important than utility.

THROUGH A GLASS DARKLY

It's all well and good to have a bottle nearby but wine wouldn't be the same without the following items.

a) SCC REWORK
b) GNAWS ISLE
c) DNA CRETE
d) CHEMISE CEO SEEN

Answer on page 155.

Answer on page 155.

THE BOTTLE OF THE MARNE

One day, far, far away in the 1950s in a land called the Costa Brava, a young and hopelessly naive student called Michael Grylls discovered fresh tasting Spanish sparkling wine and decided to market it as 'Spanish Champagne'. Pursued by French suppliers, in 1958 he ended up on the receiving end of a criminal prosecution for fraudulent mis-labelling under the Merchandise Marks Act. The judge, who was probably mindful of the long memories of the Champagne producers, cunningly summed up in favour of the industry. He reckoned, however, without the traditional anti-French antipathy of the jury, who found in favour of the Costa Brava Wine Company.

Naturally, the French suspected a British government plot to destroy their Champagne industry just as the UK was about to enter the EEC. Some bars in Paris refused to serve Scotch whisky and

the intransigent Pyreneans turned a consignment of Costa bubbly back. After an attempt at intervention by the French embassy failed, the French producers sued Grylls in 1960 for producing 'Champagne' that did not genuinely come from the region and was not made by the Champagne method.

Some French newspapers called this the 'second Battle of the Marne' and ordered the Costa Brava Wine Company to obliterate all mention of the word 'Champagne' from its labels within 48 hours. Since then, the producers of the Champagne region have kept an extremely vigilant watch on their mark.

In 1975, with a complete sense of humour failure, they obtained an injunction from the makers of Babycham, stopping them from calling it 'Champagne perry'.

114

HIDDEN GEMS

The following countries and states are lesser-known producers of wine:

All 50 of the United States of America,
as well as the District of Columbia (Washington DC)
Brazil · China
Georgia (the country and the State)
India · Japan · Kenya
Lebanon · Libya
Syria · Thailand
Tunisia · Ukraine · Uruguay

WORDS ON WINE

GRAPE, *n.*
Hail noble fruit! – by Homer sung,
Anacreon and Khayyam;
Thy praise is ever on the tongue
Of better men than I am.
The lyre in my hand has never swept,
The song I cannot offer:
My humbler service pray accept –
I'll help to kill the scoffer.
The water-drinkers and the cranks
Who load their skins with liquor –
I'll gladly bear their belly-tanks
And tap them with my sticker.
Fill up, fill up, for wisdom cools
When e'er we let the wine rest.
Here's death to Prohibition's fools,
And every kind of vine-pest!

**Jamrach Holobom, quoted in
Ambrose Bierce's,** *The Devil's Dictionary* **(1911)**

WHEN MARTINIS JUST AREN'T DE RIGUEUR

Bond's wines: Taittinger

It's the literary James bond who goes in for Taittinger – in the novel of *Casino Royale* (1953), he drinks Taittinger Brut Blanc de Blancs '43, while in the book *Moonraker* (aka *Too Hot to Handle*, 1955) he dismisses Taittinger as 'a fad' of his. In *On Her Majesty's Secret Service* (1963), he orders a bottle of Blanc de Blancs to his room in the Hotel Splendide. In the film of *From Russia with Love* (1963), Red Grant slips Tatiana a Taittinger mickey, while David Niven later drinks it aboard Woody Allen's aircraft in the underrated film *Casino Royale* (1967).

WINE VOCABULARY 101

Learn these terms and you'll be able to bluff with the best of them...

Acidic: tart, sour

Balance: the equilibrium of a wine's 'ingredients' – ie acid, sugar, tannin, alcohol – all of which should complement but not overwhelm each other

Botrytis cinerea: also known as noble rot, the Latin name for one of the moulds which can attack grapes on the vine; in ideal conditions, the mould will remove much of the juice from the wine and leave a sweet pulp that is then pressed to make fabulous dessert wines such as Sauternes and Tokaji (or Tokay)

Chewy: literally, a wine that gives you the need to chew a little bit – a dry feeling on the back of your teeth which can come from high-but-balanced acidic wine with significant tannins

Dry: no noticeable sweetness – technically, a dry wine is one in which all the sugar has been fermented out

Finish: aftertaste – the amount of time the flavour lasts after the wine has been swallowed; described as long, short or medium-length

Malolactic fermentation: a conversion by bacteria of the malic acid present in grapes, into lactic acid which generally lowers the acidity – this sometimes results in a creamy, buttery character

Varietal: synonym for grape variety – or when describing wine, a single variety

'WAITER, WAITER, THERE'S A SNAKE PENIS IN MY WINE'

In Guangzhou province, China, you are very likely to find some genuine snake wines that many people claim to actually enjoy. These slippery little suckers are immersed in 100% rice wine in special glass bottles and then sealed and stored in a cellar for five years. Claiming to be high quality tonics which can produce a range of benefits from improved skin to straightened bones, tendons and muscles, they are used to treat general fatigue, hair loss, migraine, headaches, rheumatism and neurasthenia.

Most of the snakes are poisonous. If that isn't enough of a thrill for you, try snake penis wine, full of hundreds of little snake peckers. This is the one to go for if you need to banish fatigue, strengthen the waist, invigorate the kidneys, nourish the yin to produce semen, reinforce the vital essence, control sexual disorders like impotence, or 'control nocturnal emission'.

Now there remains only the simple matter of actually drinking it.

WINE WORDS

Bull's Blood

Hungarian Bikaver wine, made near the town of Eger, is a strong, dark brick-red wine. The Spanish have their own rendition called Sangre de Toro. Farther afield, Chianti's great varietal — Sangiovese — means 'the blood of Jove'. Likewise, from the French, there's a process called *saigneé*, meaning 'bleeding off', when a percentage of red wine juice from the fermenting must is used to intensify fruit flavours. On a more squeamish note, real bull's blood was commonly used to clarify wine (a process called fining, which removes impurities) until the EU banned the use of animal products in 1997 as part of the fight against BSE.

Speaking of body parts — eyes feature in several wine names. Another name for the Tempranillo of Spain is Ull de Lebre, 'eye of the hare'. And the best vin santo (sweet Italian wine made from air-dried grapes) is called Occhio di Pernice ('eye of the partridge').

SAY IT WITH SANGRIA

Every country has its version of a wine-based, alcohol-fortified fruit punch; Spain's, called Sangria, is possibly the most well-known. Traditionally made with Rioja (red), there is such a drink as Sangria Blanco, made with white wine, and even a sparkling version made with Cava. Sangria is typically made from some combination of the following: red wine; fruit juice; fruit-flavoured soda; brandy or other spirit; and various other ingredients. When making your own Sangria, use as good quality a red wine as you can muster, preferably Rioja, and if possible let it chill well overnight.

Here's one recipe for a crowd, courtesy of Ignacio Villalgordo:

Ingredients:
Red wine – young, fruity and powerful preferred, 1 bottle for each litre of soda.
Soda – lemon and orange (use half and half), Fanta if possible.
Red Vermouth – preferably Martini Rosso, 1 bottle for every 10l of Sangria)
A glass of Cointreau.
Plenty of fresh fruit – orange, lemon, peach and apricot (indispensable!),
you can also add banana, pineapple or melon.
Cinnamon and sugar to taste.

Preparation:
- The day before, make a big block of ice (or more). Tip: use a plastic container (Tupperware or similar). That way you can chill the sangria without watering it down. It's also advisable to pre-chill all the liquids (wine, Fanta, etc.).

- Dice the fruit - not too big - about 1.5 centimetres to avoid big chunks filling the glasses.

- Put the fruit in a big container together with a bottle of wine, sugar, ground cinnamon and some of the soda. Soak for an hour. After that, add the rest of ingredients, correct sugar and cinnamon to taste (apparently cinnamon is an aphrodisiac, so plenty of it!). Add the ice and ¡Salud!

Optional improvement:
Add the fresh juice of two oranges and half a lemon.

IT'S THE WINE TALKING

Hit your wine merchant across the mouth when, innocently trying to put you on to a good thing, or what he sees as one, he recommends you to 'buy for laying down'.
Rule 7 of 'The Wine Resenter's Handy Guide',
in *On Drink* (1972) by Kingsley Amis

There are some times when a screwcap would be better...

KNOCK IT ON THE HEAD

We all know what a hangover feels like – headache, nausea, diarrhoea, lack of appetite, shakiness and feeling tired and unwell being the common symptoms. But a new dual-action hangover cure called Sober Up from Bhelliom Enterprises, aims to knock out a hangover before it starts or to relieve one the next day.

Take two tablets of Sober Up with RYVOX-9 when you've finished drinking and you'll wake up the next morning without a hangover, claim the manufacturers.

Or, if you already have a hangover, the same 30-minute recovery rule will apply.

The tablets are said to work with your body's natural alcohol detoxification system to quickly and safely metabolise alcohol and its by-product, Acetaldehyde, so as to prevent a hangover.

MEN OF KENT

Anyone who has visited the bleak wastes around the Romney Marsh coastline can see why it was particularly suitable for eighteenth century smuggling. These bleak shores, like similarly wild terrain in Cornwall, Devon, East Cleveland and Sussex, became the scene for what was a huge industry and almost an eighteenth century national pastime.

The illegal landing of wine, tea, brandy and other goods high in indirect taxation was highly profitable, and probably accounted for as much income as legitimate trade. John Wesley (1703–1791) wrote somewhat sadly that the people were 'receptive to his teachings but unwilling to give up smuggling'.

Smuggling was also a two-way traffic across the channel and Romney Marsh wool was smuggled across to France in large volumes, continuing well into the nineteenth century. Small boats met the big ships from France about three miles out and brought the contraband ashore where huge numbers of men – up to 1,000 in many cases – scrabbled to earn a week's wage for carrying the kegs up the beach to the hiding place. Between 1723 and 1733, some 250 customs men were killed or beaten up. It became so common that fines were standardised with £40 being charged for a wounded excise man and £100 for a dead one.

IN X-CESS

The only word to describe partying in Kiev 100 years ago is 'respect'. The drinkers often became so excitable after a heavy session that unorthodox drinking games like 'Venera', or 'Venus', abounded. In this game, a naked girl was laid out, decorated with flowers and appetisers. The appearance of this dish caused ecstasy among the drinkers, who would grab a bottle of Champagne and pop their corks towards the ceiling.

Patrons would make toasts to the nubile young girl, pour Champagne over her and stick different banknotes to her body, then dig in to the snacks adorning her, at 90 roubles per head for two hours of the 'big show.' It was not uncommon to fork out 4,500 roubles for the whole party – an astronomical sum when the average clerk earned 100 roubles a month.

Other 'dishes' included the 'Dance of Odalisques on Tables around Dishes', 'Mermaids Bathing in Champagne' and 'Live Roman Swing' where drunken clients would swing naked women, often dropping them. One form of entertainment, the Aquarium, particularly delighted the assembled wags. The top of a piano was removed and filled with several dozen bottles of Champagne and fish from the Dnipro river, while the piano player kept time with a merry melody.

ALL GREEK TO ME

Nowadays we think of a symposium as a rather earnest gathering of experts to discuss weighty matters. But the original was something rather different. The symposium in Ancient Greece was the ancient equivalent of going down the pub. It literally means 'a drinking together' where men lay on couches and quaffed rather than sipped wine. Rather like Japanese businessmen enjoying a Geisha party, they drank deeply, engaged in chit-chat and watched a floor-show. Women, needless to say, were not invited to this origin of the toga party.

Socrates' comment on the symposium sums up its delights nicely: 'So far as drinking is concerned, gentlemen, you have my approval. Wine moistens the souls and lulls our grief to sleep while it also awakens kindly feelings. Yet I suspect men's bodies react like those of growing plants. When a god gives plants too much water to drink they can't stand up straight and the winds flatten them, but when they drink exactly what they require, they grow straight and tall and bear abundant fruit, and so it is with us.'

THUNDERBIRDS ARE GONE!

Billed as 'The American Classic', 17.5% alcohol by volume Thunderbird wine is actually made and bottled by the reputable E&J Gallo Winery in Modesto, CA, yet it cannot shake off its association with heavy drinking.

Often known as 'T-Bird', the history of Thunderbird is as interesting as the drunken effects experienced from the wine. Aficionados say that these include raging hangovers and a mysterious chemical reaction that causes the light yellow liquid to turn your tongue black, as if you have been chewing on hearty lumps of charcoal.

Allegedly, when prohibition ended, Ernest Gallo and his brothers Julio and Joe wanted to corner the young wine market to become 'the Campbell soup of the wine industry'. So they started selling Thunderbird with a radio advertisement that featured the song:

> 'What's the word?
> Thunderbird.
> How's it sold?
> Good and cold.
> What's the jive?
> Bird's alive.
> What's the price?
> Thirty twice.'

GO ON, HAVE ANOTHER GLASS

The most expensive meal ever eaten at a restaurant – solely because of the wine – came to £44,000. The 2001 dinner at London's Pétrus restaurant included five bottles of wine, a 1947 Château Pétrus (£12,300); a 1945 Château Pétrus (£11,600); a 1946 Château Pétrus (£9,400 – apparently at cost); a 1900 Château d'Yquem (£9,200); and a 1982 Montrachet (£1,400). The remainder was spent on water, cigarettes, Champagne and a tip. The restaurant generously waived the £300 charge for the food. Five of the six bankers who ran up this bill were ultimately sacked over the bad publicity.

GOES DOWN SMOOTHLY

Wine is a very sexy drink: it has body, aroma, legs, mouth, feel… It can be complex, firm, hot and volatile. Not to mention all that racking and pumping that goes on in production… Here are some of the sexiest wines…

Le Pin – full bodied, rich, voluptuous and fleshy

Krug Rosé – an expensive redhead

Saint-Amour – the only wine to drink on Valentine's Day

Penfolds Grange – the Pamela Anderson of Australian Shiraz: lots of make up, and big…

Pinot Noir – the drink of Mother Earth herself

Madeira – the perfect seduction wine ('Have some Madeira, m'dear.')

Château La Fleur du Gay – from one man to another, with love

Flowers, Sonoma – nice bouquet…

Clos de Tart – only for the truly desperate

Puligny-Montrachet 1er Cru Les Demoiselles – hello, laydeeezzz

Mondavi's Byron Vineyard – Romantic poet, romantic wine

Darling, South Africa – aahhh

ALL GREEK TO ME

The wine-fuelled madness of Dionysos gave birth to theatre as we know it. In the sixth century BC large choruses of young men, around 50 in number, would gather to sing spontaneous songs in praise of the god of drunkenness and creativity. Gradually they began to deal with myths and legends, and participants would dress up and wear animal skins to represent what they were singing about. These songs were known as dithyrambs. By the fifth century dithyramb competitions were being held, and gradually they evolved into a chorus exchanging a dramatic sung monologue with a soloist. This is why Greek tragedy always has a chorus – they were the singers of the dithyramb.

Gradually two then three solo performers were introduced, and theatre as we know it was born, but dithyrambs continued to be composed and performed alongside more theatrical works. We have a small number of examples from the fifth century by poets like Bacchylides and Timotheus of Miletus.

HAVE A NICE GLASS OF BASTARD

Due to their damp climate, the English liked strong dessert wines to warm them up, and in the fourteenth century, a sweet Spanish wine called Bastard found favour. A poem from the time commemorates the variety of wines available:

> *'Ye shall have Rumney and Malmsyne*
> *Both Hippocras and Vernage wine,*
> *Mount Rose and the wines of Greke*
> *Both Algrade and despice eke*
> *Antioche and Bastarde*
> *Pyment also and Garnarde:*
> *Wine of Greek and Muscadell,*
> *Both clare, pyment and Rochell.'*

COOK-IN SAUCE

In Roman cooking most food was served with a sauce, usually spicy or piquant, designed to cover up the taste of less than perfectly preserved ingredients. Apicius even gives a special recipe for 'high' poultry, ie rotting birds. There were three basic types of wine sauce: those made with sweet wine, to which honey was often also added; those made with ordinary wine, where wine provided the main liquid; and the rest, which usually featured some wine and wine vinegar along with other liquid such as stock. Very few sauces escaped the tilting of the bottle.

To our taste many of these sauces would be overpowering, combining as they do salty fish essence, pepper, cumin, rosemary, cloves, almonds, dates and raisins. Even very delicately flavoured fish and vegetables were stewed in wine, wine vinegar, honey and all manner of spices.

Despite this we can recognise the roots of much of our twentieth century cooking in what the Romans were doing. They steamed mussels and served them with a sauce made from the cooking liquid with white wine, chives and cumin added, and marinaded their pork chops in a mixture of chicken stock and red wine with black pepper and cumin, before frying them off until golden brown. They made hot mint sauce from wine, vinegar and olive oil, sweetened with honey, and served it with mutton, and eggs poached in seasoned red wine.

THROUGH A GLASS DARKLY

Which of the following is not a member of the Vitis Vinifera species of 'Old World' grapes that originated in what is now Iran.

a) Folle Blanche
b) Muscadine
c) Gewurztraminer
d) Bual

Answer on page 155.

Answer on page 155.

'ERE IAGO

Poor old Cassio. There he is in *Othello*, seduced by Iago into taking a drink in order to involve him in a quarrel and he finds himself much the worse for wear and regretting his actions:

Cassio: O God, that men should put an enemy in their mouths to steal away their brains! That we should, with joy, pleasance, revel and applause, transform ourselves into beasts!

Iago: Why, but you are well enough: how came you thus recovered?

Cassio: It hath pleased the devil drunkenness to give place to the devil wrath; one unperfectness shows me another, to make me frankly despise myself.

Iago: Come, you are too severe a moraler: as the time, the place, and the condition of this country stands, I could heartily wish this had not befallen; but since it is as it is, mend it for your own good.

Cassio: I will ask him for my place again: he shall tell me I am a drunkard! Had I as many mouths as a Hydra, such an answer would stop them all. To be now a sensible man, by and by a fool, and presently a beast! O strange! Every inordinate cup is unblessed and the ingredient is a devil.

Iago: Come, come, good wine is a good familiar creature if it is well used; exclaim no more against it.

IT'S THE WINE TALKING

Despair is vinegar from the wine of hope.
Austin O'Malley, American humourist

WORDS ON WINE

Eleven--twelve--one o'clock had struck, and the gentlemen had not arrived. Consternation sat on every face. Could they have been waylaid and robbed? Should they send men and lanterns in every direction by which they could be supposed likely to have travelled home? or should they--Hark! There they were. What could have made them so late? A strange voice, too! To whom could it belong? They rushed into the kitchen, whither the truants had repaired, and at once obtained rather more than a glimmering of the real state of the case.

Mr. Pickwick, with his hands in his pockets and his hat cocked completely over his left eye, was leaning against the dresser, shaking his head from side to side, and producing a constant succession of the blandest and most benevolent smiles without being moved thereunto by any discernible cause or pretence whatsoever; old Mr. Wardle, with a highly-inflamed countenance, was grasping the hand of a strange gentleman muttering protestations of eternal friendship; Mr. Winkle, supporting himself by the eight-day clock, was feebly invoking destruction upon the head of any member of the family who should suggest the propriety of his retiring for the night; and Mr. Snodgrass had sunk into a chair, with an expression of the most abject and hopeless misery that the human mind can imagine, portrayed in every lineament of his expressive face.

'Is anything the matter?' inquired the three ladies.

'Nothing the matter,' replied Mr. Pickwick. 'We--we're--all right.--I say, Wardle, we're all right, ain't we?'

'I should think so,' replied the jolly host.--'My dears, here's my friend Mr. Jingle--Mr. Pickwick's friend, Mr. Jingle, come 'pon--little visit.'

'Is anything the matter with Mr. Snodgrass, Sir?' inquired Emily, with great anxiety.

'Nothing the matter, ma'am,' replied the stranger. 'Cricket dinner--glorious party--capital songs--old Port--claret--good--very good--wine, ma'am--wine.'

'It wasn't the wine,' murmured Mr. Snodgrass, in a broken voice. 'It was the salmon.' Somehow or other, it never is the wine, in these cases.

Charles Dickens,
The Pickwick Papers **(1837)**

'Sir, I am told this is a big wine.'

VENI VEDI VINO

They came, they saw, they drank. The Roman philosophers were fond of a glass or three of wine. Ovid reckoned that 'Wine gives courage and makes men apt for passion.' Pliny's comment has endured over the centuries: 'In vino veritas' – in wine is truth.

HOW TO REMOVE A WINE LABEL

While a digital camera helps preserve the memory of a fabulous wine, there's nothing like having the label itself. There are several products on the market for removing labels – variations of a plastic sheet with strong adhesive on one side – but all you really need is a soap and water. Fill a bucket with lukewarm water and a small amount of dish-washing liquid, and plunk the bottle in overnight. If the glue on the back of the label is water soluble, the label should peel right off. If it's not water soluble, you'll need a razor blade to carefully work the label off. Let the labels dry on a sunny window-sill or towel resting on a radiator. They tend to curl, you can flatten them later.

IT'S THE WINE TALKING

It actually comes down to what thrills you.
Hugh Johnson, world-renowned wine writer

GREAT WINE RECIPES

Champagne sorbet

You can make Champagne sorbet by complex methods, or you can make it by simple ones. There seems no good reason not to stick to the straightforward method, which says combine Champagne, lemons and sugar and churn.

Juice three lemons, pour in a bottle of dry Champagne (anything too expensive would be a waste, the cold takes away the more subtle flavours) and stir in eight ounces of caster sugar until dissolved. Pour into an ice cream maker and churn. Don't worry if it seems to be taking a long time, the alcohol retards freezing. This is a recipe that really can't be made by using a normal freezer and periodically whipping, as it relies on the smoothness of the sorbet for effect.

A particularly nice way to serve it as boozy desert, if you can lay your hands on some Marc de Champagne spirit, is to souse two scoops of sorbet in a tablespoon of the fiery spirit before serving.

WORDS ON WINE

It is wrong to say that Americans will not talk at their meals. I never met but few who would not talk to me, at any rate till I got to the far West; but I have rarely found that they would address me first. Then the dinner comes early – at least it always does so in New England – and the ceremony is much of the same kind. You came there to eat, and the food is pressed upon you ad nauseam. But, as far as one can see, there is no drinking. In these days, I am quite aware that drinking has become improper, even in England. We are apt, at home, to speak of wine as a thing tabooed, wondering how our fathers lived and swilled. I believe that, as a fact, we drink as much as they did; but, nevertheless, that is our theory. I confess, however, that I like wine. It is very wicked, but it seems to me that my dinner goes down better with a glass of sherry than without it. As a rule, I always did get it at hotels in America. But I had no comfort with it.

Sherry they do not understand at all. Of course I am only speaking of hotels. Their claret they get exclusively from Mr. Gladstone, and, looking at the quality, have a right to quarrel even with Mr. Gladstone's price. But it is not the quality of the wine that I hereby intend to subject to ignominy so much as the want of any opportunity for drinking it. After dinner, if all that I hear be true, the gentlemen occasionally drop into the hotel bar and 'liquor up.' Or rather this is not done specially after dinner, but, without prejudice to the hour, at any time that may be found desirable. I also have 'liquored up,' but I cannot say that I enjoy the process. I do not intend hereby to accuse Americans of drinking much; but I maintain that what they do drink, they drink in the most uncomfortable manner that the imagination can devise.

Anthony Trollope,
North America **(1862)**

DRINK LIKE AN EGYPTIAN

Some of the earliest recorded references to wine are by the Egyptians – in their tomb paintings and the wine jars found in excavated tombs. While wild grapes never grew in ancient Egypt, a flourishing wine industry developed along the fertile Nile Delta – probably as a result of trade between Egypt and Palestine – by 2700BC). By the end of the 'Old Kingdom' period, it was traditional for mummies to be buried with five types of wine for the afterlife. Talk about ageing potential.

HOW TO RECOGNISE VINOUS CARICATURES

The Chardonnay Girl

Though out with the girls for a good time, she's acutely aware of how she looks to the rest of the room. Pubs are so dirty and smelly, she prefers the vaguely Scandinavian, blonde wood atmosphere of an airy wine bar. She'll drink wine, rather than beer, as it's less filling – plus it's sophisticated and supposedly more healthy. She is brand-conscious and sticks to the familiar.

IT'S THE WINE TALKING

We want the finest wines available to humanity,
we want them here, and we want them now!
Withnail, played by Richard E Grant in *Withnail and I* (1987)

CHAMPERS PAMPERS

For many people, bathing in Champagne is a sign of ultimate decadence. We can't imagine it cleans very well, figure it would sting on freshly shaved areas, and must leave a sticky residue, but each to their own. Dame Nellie Melba, Aussie opera singer and well known diva, wasn't complaining when her neighbour, Seppelt winemaker Hans Irvine, offered her a bath in 152 bottles of his best fizz.

According to the Seppelt legend Dame Nellie happened to wonder out loud in his hearing – and if you believe that you'll believe anything – what it would be like to bath in Champagne. Irvine duly ordered his workers to carry a bath into the vaults, screen it off and fill it up. Dame Nellie had her bath, complaining it was a little chilly, and then off she went, leaving the workers to clear up the mess. So they decided, with an eye on the souvenir hunter's market no doubt, to bottle the special vintage. The only thing was, when they'd emptied the last drop, they found they'd filled 153 bottles, one more than they originally poured in.

POP GOES THE BUBBLY

Champagne (and all sparkling wine) is bottled under tremendous pressure, and releasing the cork safely and confidently takes a little practice. Though the famous cork popping sound is part of a tradition of sorts, here is the safer, more sophisticated, and less wasteful way to open a bottle.

1. Remove foil from the cork.
2. Untwist the wire 'basket' (experts say it should be removable with five and a half twists).
3. Wrap the neck of the bottle and cork in a dish cloth.
4. Angle the bottle at about 45 degrees, and away from you (and your guests).
5. Hold the cork firmly through the towel and gently turn the bottle.
6. Slowly withdraw the cork out of neck, you'll hear a little pop and then see a lovely wisp of vapour.

A RED GIVEAWAY

There's only one problem with enjoying a nice bottle of red wine in the middle of the week – everyone else can see what you've been up to. It's one of the worst culprits for staining teeth, and has a nasty habit of turning your tongue and any rough skin on your lips purple. The higher the tannins, the more tenacious the stain. So what can you do?

Giving up the wine is obviously out of the question, so we suggest:

- Carry lip salve with you. Not only will it protect your lips to a certain extent, if you get into the habit of applying it regularly then your nice smooth smacker will be less likely to stain in the first place.
- Switch to using a mild whitening toothpaste daily.
- If you're on a big date, then consider sneaking one of the new tongue-scraper toothbrushes into your pocket and slipping off to brush and buff after each couple of glasses. Alternatively carry a few GoSMILE Dalies (sadly only available in America) – £15 ($28) gets you seven doses of this 'anywhere, anytime, no water needed' tooth-whitening system in a sleek silver carrying case.

JUST TO CLARIFY

This tasting note for Lustau 'Los Arcos' Dry Amontillado Sherry is a homage to David Foster Wallace, a contemporary writer whose footnotes are always far lengthier than the text to which they refer. This review is provided with permission of BasicJuice.com

Lustau[1] 'Los Arcos'[2] Dry[3] Amontillado Sherry ($10) – Very bright[4] caramel/copper in color. This Sherry offers dizzying[5] scents of roasted almond[6], salt[7], date[8], and wood[9]. In the mouth, The Arcs[10] tastes like a dry Tawny Port[11]. This is a tasty wine[12], wrapped up[13] in a tangy, food-friendly[14] package[15]. Sip[16] Los Arcos alongside your favorite *tapa*[17]. It is the perfect accompaniment to Gazpacho[18].

(1) Lustau was actually established in 1896[a] by Don Jose Ruiz-Berdejo y Veyan. I've no idea why the brand isn't named 'Ruiz-Berdejo y Veyan,' unless it simply costs too much in terms of label real estate or ink outlay.

(2) Or 'The Arcs' if you have limited or no command[b] of the Spanish language.

(3) And when the Spanish designate Sherry as 'dry,' they aren't whistling Dixie[c]. There will be precisely zero fruit scents, aromas or flavors to be pried[d] out of the glass.

(4) I'm not implying the wine actually glows in the dark. Rather it shimmers in the glass. Perhaps the description should have read, 'Shiny, shimmering[e] caramel and/or copper in color.'

(5) When sniffed or drunk in moderation, Sherry does not cause dizziness. It is dizzying in the sense that the mind struggles to conjure up adjectives for all the volatile molecules ascending the nasal passages and making contact with cilia-equipped neurons.

(6) Preheat oven to 350°F[f]. Spread almonds over baking sheet. Roast for twenty minutes or until almond skin begins to crack.

(7) Many Sherry producers and enthusiasts claim that Sherry grapevines are imbued with salt from ocean spray carried on the breeze[g].

(8) Fruit of the date palm (*Phoenix dactylifera*), which is mentioned in both the Koran and Bible[h].

(9) This is one of those annoying adjectives used by wine writers the world over. I don't mean that the wine smells like a plank of wood. Rather, it smells like the inside of a toasted barrel[i]. Of course, not many folks have actually sniffed the inside of a barrel, let alone a toasted barrel.

(10) On-demand Spanish translation!

(11) To my knowledge, there is no such thing as a dry Tawny Port[j]. Tawny Ports are actually quite sweet. Their unique flavors can be partially attributed to wood (see [9])

(12) One of the major struggles in wine

writing is avoiding repetition when referring to the wine under review. I'm tapped out after, 'this wine,' 'the wine,' 'this Sherry,' and 'Los Arcos.' I now must resort to inserting adjectives such as 'this tasty wine.' Redundancy is a killer.

(13) The reader is being set up here for a whopper[k] of a metaphor. I am attempting to paint a mental image of the Sherry as a gift, wrapping paper and all.

(14) Another all-too-commonplace wine adjective.

(15) Metaphor delivered[l].

(16) While sipping isn't required, it is recommended. Los Arcos tastes deceptively light in the alcohol department. However, it packs an alcohol-punch of 18.5% [m].

(17) *Tapa* literally means 'cover' or 'lid [n].'

(18) A cold[o], tomato-based Spanish soup that is popular in warmer areas and during the summer. It is usually spicy, but a milder variant has also become popular.

(a) Also the year in which Utah was granted statehood.

(b) And really, shouldn't we all learn Spanish as a sign of friendship to our southern (as in Mexico) neighbors?

(c) Or whatever ditty your typical Spaniard might whistle.

(d) **pry** *tr.v.* pried, prying, pries

(e) Thus I would have been able to employ the timeless literary device of alliteration, which is clearly illustrated by the phrase, 'Sally sells seashells by the seashore.'

(f) $Tc = (^5/_9)*(Tf-32)$; Tc = temperature in degrees Celsius, Tf = temperature in degrees Fahrenheit

(g) This needn't be a Wizard of Oz-type breeze. The Sherry region is, in fact, on the southern coast of Spain. So there is close proximity to ocean spray, although I'm not sure if I buy the whole salt-imbued-vineyard thing.

(h) And, I assume, the Torah.

(i) Barrels are often toasted on the inside for purposes of ageing wine. The toasted wood imparts buttery, spicy-sweet scents to aging wine.

(j) Tawny Port is aged in wooden barrels, exposing it to gradual oxidation and evaporation, causing its color to mellow to a golden-brown after roughly ten years 'in wood'.

(k) As in a large-sized, heavy-duty metaphor – not a big hamburger or malted chocolate candy.

(l) !!

(m) A higher alcohol percentage than even the biggest of California Cabernet or Zinfandel wines.

(n) The association with appetizers is thought to have come from the old habit of placing a slice of bread or a piece of ham on top of one's wine glass, perhaps to keep out insects. This edible lid was the precursor of modern-day *tapas*.

(o) In both fiction and real life, there have occurred embarrassing situations in which a Gazpacho-ignorant diner insists that his or her cold soup be heated up.

STONE DRUNK

About the same time as Stonehenge was built, give or take a few centuries, our ancestors may have been debating the merits of 'Chateau Hajji Firuz', the nickname given to a yellowish residue found inside a nine-litre jar excavated by Mary M Voigt from a site the northern Zagros Mountains of Iran. The site dates from 5400–5000BC.

THROUGH A GLASS DARKLY

Which of the following is the 'flagship' grape of Chile?
a) Carmenère
b) Merlot
c) Carmelo
d) Garnacha
Answer on page 155.

ERSTWHILE VINOUS VOCAB

Terms that have fallen from favour (but perhaps shouldn't have...)

Nipperkin: A small wine and beer measure. Now called a 'nip'.

Bastard: Any sweetened wine, but more correctly a sweet Spanish wine (white or brown) made of the bastard muscadine grape. 'I will pledge you willingly in a cup of bastard.' – from *Kenilworth*, Sir Walter Scott (1821). (NB: Bastardo is also a grape variety.)

Widow's Port: A wine sold for port, but of quite a different family. As a widow retains her husband's name after he dies, so a mixture of potato spirit and inferior wine retains the name of port, though every drop of port is taken from it.

Shades: Wine vaults. The Brighton Old Bank, in 1819, was turned by Mr Savage into a smoking-room and ginshop. There was an entrance to it by the Pavilion Shades, and Savage took down the word bank, and inserted the word shades. This term was not inappropriate, as the room was in reality shaded by the opposite house, occupied by Mrs Fitzherbert.

Source: Brewer's Dictionary of Phrase and Fable *(1898)*

BUBBLING OVER WITH TRIVIA

Champagne is indeed an amazing drink... but did you know:

- Chilling Champagne helps reduce the pressure tremendously.
- The word Champagne comes from the Roman for 'campania', or field.
- The Romans dug material for buildings and highways out of the chalk in the Champagne region, leaving miles of caves, called 'crayères' – some as deep as 300ft. These have since sheltered millions of bottles of Champagne.
- Over 330 million bottles of Champagne are produced each year.
- The wire 'basket' that covers the cork is called a muselet.
- Until 1850, all Champagne was sweet.
- One quarter of the British drink four times as much Champagne each year as does the entire population of the US.
- Dirt produces bubbles – dust particles in the glass, or strands from the dish towel used to dry it, encourages more vigorous bubbles
- The longest recorded Champagne cork flight was 177ft, 9in (53,32m), 4ft (1,2m) from ground level at Woodbury Vineyards in New York State
- Champagne can only be called Champagne if it comes from the Champagne region of France and is made in the traditional way, from sanctioned grape varieties. (But you probably know that by now.)

WINE WORDS

Hock

This slang term for German white wine – short for the obsolete word hock-amore (a botched form of Hochheimer, after the German town Hochheim-on-the-Main) – was in use well before Queen Victoria and her German husband Prince Albert visited the region in 1845. In fact the wine, abbreviated HOCK, was being shipped to England in boatloads. But it became that much more popular following the royal couple's invitation to a tasting hosted by one vineyard owner, GM Papstmann, who was granted the honour of calling his vineyard 'Königin Victoriaberg' in 1850. Like claret is to Bordeaux, hock is now a generic term for (mainly cheap) German wine.

WORDS ON WINE

I was interested in Californian wine. Indeed, I am interested in all wines, and have been all my life, from the raisin wine that a school-fellow kept secreted in his play-box up to my last discovery, those notable Valtellines, that once shone upon the board of Caesar.

Some of us, kind old Pagans, watch with dread the shadows falling on the age: how the unconquerable worm invades the sunny terraces of France, and Bordeaux is no more, and the Rhone a mere Arabia Petraea. Château Neuf is dead, and I have never tasted it; Hermitage – a hermitage indeed from all life's sorrows – lies expiring by the river. And in the place of these imperial elixirs, beautiful to every sense, gem-hued, flower-scented, dream-compellers:- behold upon the quays at Cette the chemicals arrayed; behold the analyst at Marseilles, raising hands in obsecration, attesting god Lyoeus, and the vats staved in, and the dishonest wines poured forth among the sea. It is not Pan only; Bacchus, too, is dead.

If wine is to withdraw its most poetic countenance, the sun of the white dinner-cloth, a deity to be invoked by two or three, all fervent, hushing their talk, degusting tenderly, and storing reminiscences - for a bottle of good wine, like a good act, shines ever in the retrospect – if wine is to desert us, go thy ways, old Jack! Now we begin to have compunctions, and look back at the brave bottles squandered upon dinner-parties, where the guests drank grossly, discussing politics the while, and even the schoolboy 'took his whack,' like liquorice water. And at the same time, we look timidly forward, with a spark of hope, to where the new lands, already weary of producing gold, begin to green with vineyards. A nice point in human history falls to be decided by Californian and Australian wines.

Wine in California is still in the experimental stage; and when you taste a vintage, grave economical questions are involved. The beginning of vine-planting is like the beginning of mining for the precious metals: the wine-grower also 'Prospects.' One corner of land after another is tried with one kind of grape after another. This is a failure; that is better; a third best. So, bit by bit, they grope about for their Clos Vougeot and Lafite. Those lodes and pockets of earth, more precious than the precious ores, that yield inimitable fragrance and soft fire; those virtuous Bonanzas, where the soil has sublimated under sun and stars to something finer, and the wine is bottled poetry: these still lie undiscovered; chaparral conceals, thicket embowers them; the miner chips the rock and wanders farther, and the grizzly muses undisturbed. But there they bide their hour, awaiting their Columbus; and nature nurses and prepares them. The smack of Californian earth shall linger on the palate of your grandson.

Robert Louis Stevenson,
The Silverado Squatters **(1883)**

IT'S THE WINE TALKING

Strategy is buying a bottle of fine wine when you take a lady out for dinner.
Tactics is getting her to drink it.
Frank Muir, English comedian and writer

'Please, sir, I want some more.'

THROUGH A GLASS DARKLY

A wine is said to be corked when...
a) it has bits of cork floating in it
b) it is sealed with a real cork closure, rather than a screwcap or plastic closure
c) it smells unpleasant
d) it has been opened once and then re-closed
Answer on page 155.

THE PAPAL SEAL

Burgundy wines have a heritage that dates back to the fourteenth and fifteenth centuries, when red Burgundy (then known as 'Beaune') and an obscure wine called San-Pourçain-sur-Sioule were deemed of equal nobility, gracing the dinner tables of both the French King and the Pope.

San-Pourçain-sur-Sioule was the most prestigious of the wines produced by the House of Bourbon. However, when a new Duke of Burgundy, Philip the Bold inherited and married the daughter of a major wine-producer, Margaret, daughter of the Duke of Flanders, he determined that Beaune should prevail.

In 1375 at a Bruges Anglo-French conference to discuss the war, which the Pope also attended, Philip dispensed the Beaune liberally. He also took care to send large amounts of Beaune to his father-in-law the Count of Flanders and to his nephew King Charles VI of France.

Determined not to be outdone, in 1395 while he was staying with the King in Paris, Philip supplied 200 casks of Beaune of the highest quality.

In the end, his canny marketing paid off and, to this day, many people view French Burgundy as the finest wine to drink, alongside Bordeaux.

IT'S THE WINE TALKING

A thousand cups of wine do not suffice when true friends meet,
but half a sentence is too much when there is no meeting of minds.
Chinese proverb

Men are like wine – some turn to vinegar, but the best improve with age.

ONE-BALLED DICTATOR

It may not have a poetic name, and it may not sound sophisticated, but the One-Balled Dictator cocktail has a special place in history.

It consists of one part Champagne mixed with five parts liebfraumilch – some recipes even specify 'cheap liebfraumilch'. The addition of a slug of Galliano makes it into a Mussolini. Everything should be shaken together vigorously and served in a tumbler.

The One-Balled Dictator was first made in Cincinnati, Ohio, by members of the 82nd Airborne Division when they returned from World War II. A symbolic cocktail, the German wine overwhelms the French. Veterans reportedly floated a spherical cinnamon sweet in the glass to represent the single ball, inspired, no doubt, by the British wartime song 'Hitler has only got one ball, Goering has two but very small...' (to the tune of 'Colonel Bogey')

WORDS ON WINE

See Inebriety! her wand she waves,
And lo! her pale, and lo! her purple slaves!
Sots in embroidery, and sots in crape,
Of every order, station, rank, and shape:
The king, who nods upon his rattle throne;
The staggering peer, to midnight revel prone;
The slow-tongued bishop, and the deacon sly,
The humble pensioner, and gownsman dry;
The proud, the mean, the selfish, and the great,
Swell the dull throng, and stagger into state.
Lo! proud Flaminius at the splendid board,
The easy chaplain of an atheist lord,
Quaffs the bright juice, with all the gust of sense,
And clouds his brain in torpid elegance;
In china vases, see! the sparkling ill,
From gay decanters view the rosy rill;
The neat-carved pipes in silver settle laid,
The screw by mathematic cunning made:
Oh, happy priest! whose God, like Egypt's, lies
At once the deity and sacrifice.
But is Flaminius then the man alone
To whom the joys of swimming brains are known?
Lo! the poor toper whose untutor'd sense,
Sees bliss in ale, and can with wine dispense;
Whose head proud fancy never taught to steer
Beyond the muddy ecstasies of beer;
But simple nature can her longing quench,
Behind the settle's curve, or humbler bench:
Some kitchen fire diffusing warmth around,
The semi-globe by hieroglyphics crown'd;
Where canvas purse displays the brass enroll'd,
Nor waiters rave, nor landlords thirst for gold;
Ale and content his fancy's bounds confine.
He asks no limpid punch, no rosy wine;
But sees, admitted to an equal share,

Each faithful swain the heady potion bear:
Go, wiser thou! and in thy scale of taste,
Weigh gout and gravel against ale and rest;
Call vulgar palates what thou judgest so;
Say beer is heavy, windy, cold, and slow;
Laugh at poor sots with insolent pretence,
Yet cry, when tortured, where is Providence?

George Crabbe, from *Inebriety* (1775),
a spoof of Alexander Pope

FOR MEDICINAL PURPOSES ONLY

In the medieval period doctors followed the teachings of Hippocrates and Galen and treated the four humours. Like their Greek teachers they were quick to prescribe wine, which was considered a universal panacea in the Middle Ages. An old monk's prayer runs: 'He who drinks wine sleeps well. He who sleeps well cannot sin. He who does not sin goes to heaven. Amen.'

Wine wasn't just good for providing a sound night's sleep – it was also the only known antiseptic, and as such was used to disinfect cuts and scrapes and gargled with for sore throats. It was even used in crude surgery. At the time, amputations and flesh wounds were most successfully treated, although it took a lot of wine to take away the pain of having your leg hacked off, and it wasn't particularly effective at keeping away infection of the stump. However, in some operations opium was administered to stupefy the patient.

In many areas the water was undrinkable so wine and ale were habitually drunk and associated with well-being. Not that the wine was often very good. In the early monasteries it was considered an onerous part of the Mass to have to drink the wine, which meant the monks put their minds to making better wine. This is the period where the great association between monks and brewing first appears, particularly in relation to the Benedictines. Soon popular songs and ribald jokes were being made at their expense.

SECRET CELLAR SELLERS

When some Oxbridge colleges run into financial trouble, they can turn to their cellars to bail them out. Periodically the wine industry buzzes with rumours that various colleges are selling off their stock, some of it old, but often bottles less than 10 years old, which have been laid down for future generations. Kings College, Cambridge are known to have sold off 180 crates of claret at Cheffins Auction House but are rather guarded about admitting it. Others maintain that they regularly clear out their cellars via auction sales. Pity however poor New Hall, whose wine cellar consists of some 500 bottles in total, a fraction of the amount owned by colleges like Trinity.

IT'S THE WINE TALKING

If Plato is a fine red wine, then Aristotle is a dry martini.
Chet, played by Eric Stoltz in college-angst flick *Kicking and Screaming* (1995)

ALL GREEK TO ME

The amphora was a standard measure, for both the Greeks and the Romans. The Attic Greek version contained nine gallons and the Roman six.

An amphora intended for wine storage stood around four feet tall and had a circumference of around four feet, with a thin neck, three inches across, and handles at the side to make it easy to lift. It tapered down occasionally into a foot but more often into a point that could be dug into the ground or rested in a special stand sometimes employed to keep its balance.

Seals were set on the handles and stoppers by winemakers, and oblong stamps indicated the name of the official responsible and the month when the wine was bottled. Rhodes used the same seals on its amphorae as on its coin, while the jars from Thasos bore a registration mark with the vintner's name upon it, just as winemakers label their wines today.

IT'S A FACT!

- Because Cognac ages in wood, more than 19 million bottles' worth of Cognac evaporate into the air each year over Cognac, France.
- More Cognac is consumed in Hong Kong than in any other city in the world.
- France produces one fifth of all the wine made in the world.
- Although Cabernet Sauvignon is considered the Bordeaux grape, Bordeaux actually produces nearly twice as much Merlot.
- France imports more Port than any other country, about 40% of all produced.
- All the essential vitamins can be found in a glass of wine.
- Wine has so many organic chemical compounds it is considered more complex than blood serum.
- Italy produces wine in all 20 of its provinces.
- Robert Louis Stevenson referred to wine as 'bottled poetry'.
- John Wesley, the founder of the Methodist church, once said that 'wine is the noblest cordial of nature'.
- There was a time when wine was frequently prescribed in the treatment of bronchitis and influenza.
- The Languedoc region in France produces more wine than Australia.
- The Romans invented mulled wine, to make hot spring water more palatable (and hygienic)

STRICTLY FOR THE KIDS?

The Spanish equivalent of the alcopop, popularly drunk by teenagers, is *calimocho* (from the Basque *kalimotxo*, it's sometimes shortened to *kali* or *motxo*). It consists of equal measures of local red wine and Coca-Cola and is promoted by the Coca-Cola Company who distribute plastic glasses with their logo and the word *kalimotxo* on them.

Rarely served in bars, and not drunk at formal occasions, *kali* is an underground drink, mixed in litre glasses with ice added, or in part empty two-litre coke bottles. One version adds blackberry liqueur, and a spritzer variant is also drunk, which mixes white wine and fizzy lemon drinks. This alternative is known as *pitilingorri*.

HEROIC DRUNKS

Brendan Behan (1923–1964)

The immortal toper and poet Brendan Behan was born in inner-city Dublin into an educated working-class family and started life as a house painter. A sympathiser of Ogra Fianna Fail, the youth organisation generally sympathetic to the IRA, he got involved in various activities that kept him in and out of jail until 1947 – that is, being in possession of explosives for use in a planned IRA bombing campaign, attempting to murder two detectives and helping a fellow republican to escape from jail. Once out of jail himself, Behan found it impossible to tread the straight and narrow path. As a classic example, while working in Paris in 1949, he was asked to paint a sign on the window of a cafe to attract English tourists and wrote:

> *'Come in, you Anglo-Saxon swine*
> *And drink of my Algerian wine!*
> *'Twill turn your eyeballs black and blue,*
> *And damn well good enough for you!'*

Having received payment for the job, Behan fled before the cafe's proprietor had time to have the rhyme translated.

By the early 1950s he was earning a living as a writer for radio and newspapers and had gained a reputation as 'something of a character on the streets' (read: barking) in literary circles in Dublin. In fairness, Behan found fame difficult to deal with. He had long been a heavy drinker (describing himself on one occasion as 'a drinker with a writing problem') and developed diabetes in the early 1960s. This volatile combination resulted in a series of notoriously drunken public appearances, both on stage and television.

By far the most famous Irish writer of his time, he was once hired to write an advertising slogan for Guinness. As part of his payment for this the company offered him half a dozen kegs of their finest brew. After a month, the company asked Behan what he had come up with. This was a not unreasonable request given that he had managed to drink all of the beer provided. Behan's reply was uncharacteristically brief. Turning to the eager marketing executives, he grunted but a single line: 'Guinness makes you drunk.'

THROUGH A GLASS DARKLY

Which of the following is not a fortified wine?
a) Sherry
b) Vermouth
c) Recioto
d)Madeira
Answer on page 155.

WORDS ON WINE

We die of thirst more rapidly than of hunger. Men with an abundance of water, have lived for eight days without bread. Without water, the system succumbs on the fifth day.

The reason is that in starving, man tends to die of weakness; but in thirst, of a burning fever.

People are not always able to resist thirst so long. For example, in 1787, one of the hundred Swiss soldiers of Louis XVI., died from having been 24 hours without drink.

He was at a cabaret with some of his comrades, and as he was about to carry his glass to his lips, he was reproached with drinking oftener than the rest, and with not being able to do a moment without it.

He then made a bet of 10 bottles of wine, that he would not drink for 24 hours.

He ceased at once, and sat by, for two hours, seeing the others drink.

The night passed well enough, but at dawn he found it difficult to do without his habitual glass of brandy.

All the morning he was uneasy and troubled; he went hither and thither without reason, and seemed not to know what he was about.

At one o'clock he laid down, fancying he would be calmer: he was really sick, but those about him could not induce him to drink. He said he could get on till evening: he wished to gain his bet, and it is probable also, that some military pride was mingled in the matter, which prevented him from yielding to pain.

He kept up until seven o'clock, but at half—after seven was very sick and soon died, without being able to swallow a glass of wine which was presented to him.

**Jean-Anthelme Brillat-Savarin,
'Varieties of Thirst' from
Physiology of Taste (1825)**

IT'S THE WINE TALKING

I fear the man who drinks water and so remembers this morning what the rest of us said last night.
Ancient Greek proverb

THE ACID TEST

Contrary to popular belief, wine that has been sitting around for a while does not automatically turn into vinegar – it will oxidise eventually and just taste unpleasant. To make vinegar, you need an acetobacter (bacteria) or what is called a 'mother' (vinegar culture, the equivalent of a bread starter), available from home-brewing suppliers. An open bottle of vinegar stored in a warm place may also grow its own mother but it's faster just to buy some. There are various recommendations on the strength of the alcohol to use, some say you should dilute the wine with water.

- Pour a bottle of wine into a clean container (a glass container, a sterile pail, a terracotta pot).
- Add the culture to the liquid.
- Cover the container with muslin or a dish towel and secure with a rubber band or string around the rim, to allow air in but keep bugs out.
- Put the container in a dark, warm place – the warmer the location, the more quickly the bacteria will act.
- The mother should grow to a slimy, somewhat thick film over the surface. Taste test the liquid after a couple of months, using a straw to poke through the surface.
- Topping up with more alcohol will 'kill' the mother and push it to the bottom, and another will form.
- Once the wine has turned into vinegar, siphon it off and re-use some of the mother to start again.

Unsurprisingly, the best wine also makes the best vinegar...

ERSTWHILE VINOUS VOCAB

Terms that have fallen from favour (but perhaps shouldn't have...)

Supernac'ulum:

The very best wine – the word is Low Latin for 'upon the nail', meaning that the wine is so good a drinker will leave only enough in his glass to form a bead on his nail. The French say of first-class wine, 'It is fit to make a ruby on the nail' (*faire rubis sur l'ongle*). Usage: 'After a man has drunk his glass, it is usual, in the North, to turn the bottom of the cup upside down, and let a drop fall upon the thumb-nail. If the drop rolls off, the drinker is obliged to fill and drink again,' wrote Thomas Nash (in *Pierce Penilesse*, 1592). Also Bishop Hall alludes to the same custom: 'The Duke Tenterbelly... exclaims... "Let never this goodly-formed goblet of wine go jovially through me," and then he set it to his mouth, stole it off every drop, save a little remainder, which he was by custom to set upon his thumb-nail and lick off'. Also, 'This is after the fashion of Switzerland. Clear off neat, supernaculum.' – Rabelais, *Gargantua and Pantagruel* (1532–1552).

Doctor (The):

Brown sherry, so called because it is concocted from a harsh, thin wine, by the addition of old boiled mosto stock. Mosto is made by heating unfermented juice in earthen vessels, til it becomes as thick and sweet as treacle. This syrup is added to fresh 'must', and the luscious result is used for doctoring very inferior qualities of wine. (Shaw: *On Wine*). To doctor the wine. To drug it, or strengthen it with brandy. As such wines fail in aroma, connoisseurs smell at their wine. To doctor wine is to make weak wine stronger, and 'sick' wine more palatable.

Eisell:

Wormwood wine. Hamlet says to Laertes, Woul't drink up eisell – ie drink wormwood wine to show your love to the dead Ophelia? In the Troy Book of Ludgate we have the line 'Of bitter eysell and of eager [sour] wine'. And in Shakespeare's sonnets;

> *'I will drink*
> *Potions of eysell, gainst my strong infection;*
> *No bitterness that I will bitter think,*
> *Nor double penance to correct correction.'*

Source: Brewer's Dictionary of Phrase and Fable *(1898)*

HEROIC DRUNKS

Jeffrey Bernard (1932–1997)

So, farewell champion drinker and sometime swordsman Jeffrey Bernard, hero of his *Spectator* column 'Low Life' and subject of Keith Waterhouse's play *Jeffrey Bernard is Unwell*. There is a little corner of Soho's Coach and Horses that will be forever Jeffrey. The following interview extract is reprinted by kind permission of *The Idler*.

Idler: That nobility of labour thing is a ruse by the people with money to make people happy doing a shitty job.

Bernard: Well, yeah, shitty jobs are alleged to have dignity. There's nothing undignified about lying about all day and being waited on by servants, sipping bloody Champagne.

Idler: What does drinking give people?

Bernard: A cerebral kick, a lift. Confidence. The ability to chat up crumpet. Oh, to me not drinking is like being dead, almost. I sit here taking endless journeys down memory lane. It gets boring.

Idler: Have you ever been close to that before? [being a pathetic drunk]

Bernard: Once. I'm not a drunk anyway. I drink — these words are all wrong. I mean do I appear to be a nutcase to you?

Idler: No. Who called you a drunk, though?

Bernard: You did, about three minutes ago.

Idler: So, what sort of things do you think about here?

Bernard: I think about the past a lot. I'm not doing anything, am I, now? My home help sometimes takes me to the Groucho. I go there a lot because it's the nearest. Now that pubs don't exist any more.

Idler: What do you mean?

Bernard: They're awful. All pubs are terrible places now. I mean you wouldn't have known a decent pub at your age, I shouldn't think. They didn't have music. They didn't have cigarette machines. They didn't sell the chemical beer. They were for proper drinkers, not for fucking yobs, hooligans. I want to go into a pub and meet interesting people, not to look at a lot of people sitting on the floor drinking out of tins.

THROUGH A GLASS DARKLY

See if you can unravel these grape varieties.
a) NOBEL BIO – hint: it's the heart and soul of of Barolo
b) NAG CHEER – hint: the primary grape in most Southern Rhône red blends
c) ANN FED LIZ – hint: it may make some blush
d) VENEER GRILL RUNT – hint: it hears *The Sound of Music*
Answer on page 155.

Notice to our customers: you break it, you buy it.

WORDS ON WINE

Wine's a sov'reign cure for sorrow,
Let's drink to-day, and die to-morrow;
No wonder the bottle should mortals enslave,
Since it snatches the soul from the brink of the grave!

Gentle creature, hither bring,
Wine to soothe my love's despair;
Then in merry accents sing,
Woman false, as she is fair!

Wine, I say! I'll drink to madness!
Wine, my girl, to cure my sadness!
And tell me no more there is folly in drinking
Can anything equal the folly of thinking?

Magic soother! sparkling wine,
What is nectar, drink divine,
What is nectar to Champagne?
Fill the goblet! fill again!

No more, no more of am'rous folly,
From me fly black melancholy;
And tyrant take heed how you came in my view,
Lest in my distraction, your boldness you rue!

Smiling ruin, lovely woman,
Fit companion's in our wine;
For in reason surely no man
Comes within your fatal line.

Bring fresh bottles, bring fresh glasses,
From my soul how sorrow passes!
Before my witch'd eyes laughs a gay cover'd plain,
While fancy forms visions that fire my brain!

Then wine, I say! I'll drink to madness!
Wine, my girl, to cure my sadness!
And tell me no more, there's folly in drinking,
Can any thing equal the folly of thinking!

Charlotte Dacre (1782–1841),
'Wine, I Say! I'll Drink to Madness!'

IT'S THE WINE TALKING

Let us have wine and women, mirth and laughter,
Sermons and soda-water the day after.
From *Don Juan* by Lord Byron

TONGUE IN CHEEK...

In 2001, 12-year-old Annika Irmler, from Hamburg, Germany, stuck her tongue out for the record – the *Guinness Book of Records*, that is. At seven centimetres, Irmler's tongue is the longest in the world: pity she's still too young to put it to good use. Get your mind out of the gutter: with all that surface area and all those taste buds (up to 11,100 are possible) such an appendage could prove extremely useful to a wine taster: taste buds provide the ability to distinguish between different 'tastes' – salty, sweet, bitter, sour and so on.

The quantity of taste buds is hardwired into our DNA, and helps determine the type of taster we are: a 'non-taster', with the fewest taste buds; an average taster; or a super-taster. Supertasters – most of whom are women – make up about a quarter of the population, as do nontasters. The rest are average. Much more sensitive to sweet, bitter and creamy sensations, a super-taster would perceive skimmed milk as having the same creamy effect as full cream milk, and perceive the bitterness of a tannin in wine far more strongly.

Famous non-tasters include Attila the Hun and the Duke of Wellington (whose chef reportedly resigned in frustration). Famous super-tasters include Angela Mount, wine buyer for the UK's Somerfield supermarket, whose tongue was reportedly insured for £10 million.

*A meal without wine is like a
day without sunshine.*

Jean-Anthelme Brillat-Savarin

THROUGH A GLASS DARKLY

The answers. As if you needed them.

P16   c) Cava – Spain's answer to Champagne, it's traditionally made with Parellada, Xarel-lo and Macabeo grapes – though some producers are using Chardonnay. The production method is similar to that of Champagne as well.

P22   a) Sauvignon Blanc
       b) Tempranillo, the king of Spanish grapes
       c) Ugni Blanc, known in Italy as Trebbiano
       d) Sangiovese, the main grape of Chianti

P32   Neither one hit the ground: the balloon was floating over water, off the coast.

P41   Chardonnay (white)
       Pinot Noir (red)
       Pinot Meunier (red)
       Pinot Blanc (white)
       Petit Meslier (white)
       Arbanne (white)

P48   The bucket will be $^7/_{18}$ wine, and $^{11}/_{18}$ water. For example, if the smaller glass can hold 18 units, it will contain an equal amount (nine units each) of wine and water when full. The second glass – twice the size – can hold 36 units and will contain 12 units of wine and 24 units of water when full. After all the liquid is poured into the bucket, there will be 21 units of wine and 33 units of water in total – or $^{21}/_{54}$ ($^7/_{18}$) wine and $^{33}/_{54}$ ($^{11}/_{18}$) units of water.

P52   a) dry – in order to qualify as a dry wine, according to German labelling laws, the wine must contain a maximum of 0.9% residual sugar (this is the sugar left after fermentation is complete).

P54   a) St Emilion – home to such iconic French estates as Château Cheval Blanc, which belongs to fashion house LVMH (Louis Vuitton Moët Hennessy) which also happens to own Gucci.
       b) Napa Valley – Californian home of Screaming Eagle wine, a six-litre bottle of which sold for half a million dollars at auction in 2000, setting a world record.
       c) Central Otago – on New Zealand's South Island, one of the southern-most wine growing regions in the world.
       d) Piemonte – where Italy's heady Barolos are a perfect match for the truffles that grow there too.

P64   a) Pink – or to be fancy, rosé. When the skins of red Zinfandel grapes are removed just moments after pressing, the result is sweet, pink and easy to drink.
b) White or rosé. Usually made with some combination of white Chardonnay and red (actually light purple) Pinot Noir and Pinot Meunier grapes (though three others are permitted). A Champagne made entirely from Chardonnay is called a Blanc de Blancs, while one made entirely from the red grapes is called a Blanc de Noirs.
c) While the wine ranges from pale yellow to deep gold, grapes are actually a pinkish grey colour – giving away the varietal's Pinot Noir ancestry.
d) Sorry – trick question. Portugal's national tipple can be red, deep brown – even white. In fact the earlier-drinking 'cask-aged' types are named for their colour – Ruby, Tawny and White. White Port is made from white grapes such as Viosinho, Malvasia Fina, Gouveio (Verdelho), Cédega, and Rabigato, while the darker ones are made mainly from Tinto Roriz (Spain's Tempranillo); Touriga Nacional; and Touriga Franca

P73   c) Muscadet is the name of the region near Nantes, in the Loire Valley, as well as the grape variety and the white wine made from it.

P78   d) Madeira – there is no Sémillon used in the eponymous wine of the island (located between Portugal and Morocco) from which it comes.

P89   b) Dried grapes – made in several regions of Italy, harvested grapes are left to dry for several months in a room with constantly circulating air, then pressed. The juice is then sealed into a small barrel where it ferments. The result is a 'heavenly' (hence 'santo') viscous, intensely flavoured wine.

P97   Tilt the barrel gently until the liquid just touches the lip of the barrel. If they can see the bottom, then the barrel is less than half full. But if the bottom of the barrel is completely covered by wine, then it is more than half full.

P100   French for 'creamy', Crémant is a French sparkling wine made outside the Champagne region (only wine made in Champagne may be called Champagne). You'll find Crémants in Bordeaux, Alsace and Burgundy for example.

P111   a) Blossom Hill – hails from California, almost 25,000 glasses are consumed every hour.
b) Jacob's Creek – Australia's biggest wine brand and a clear front-runner in the UK, owned by Pernod Ricard.
c) Yellow Tail – owned by Australia's Casella wine; the US's favourite imported wine.

d) Lindemans – Australia's 'other' top drop; like compatriot Penfolds, Lindemans are well-known for their Bin range of numerically named wines – the newest of which are Bin 70 Chardonnay Riesling, Bin 80 Cabernet Merlot and Bin 55 Shiraz Cabernet.

P114   a) corkscrew
       b) wine glass
       c) decanter
       d) some nice cheese

P125   b) Muscadine is a member of Vitis Rotundifolia, a native North American species.

P134   a) Carmenère – originally used liberally in Bordeaux until the phylloxera outbreak in the late 1800s, Carmenère made its way to Chile, where it was 'outed' – and subsequently embraced - in the 1990s, when analysis revealed that most of what was thought to be Merlot was actually Carmenère.

P138   c) It smells unpleasant. The generic term 'corked' is one of the most misapplied descriptions. Though bona fide cork taint does exist, the wet, mouldy odour that can affect wine can come from a host of other causes, many of which occur during production and have nothing to do with the type of closure used. Better to use the term 'faulty'.

P145   c) Recioto – Another lovely Italian air-dried grape wine, it can be either sweet (simply called Recioto) or dry (called Amarone).

P149   a) Nebbiolo – Grown in a few places, it really comes into its own in Italy's Piemonte where it's used for Barolo, Barbaresco and Nebbiolo d'Alba
       b) Grenache – the world's most widely planted red grape
       c) Zinfandel – made famous by the Californian 'blush wine' craze of the 1980s, it claims the same Croatian origins as Italy's Primitivo
       d) Grüner Veltliner – hails from Austria, makes astonishingly delicate whites

God made only water, but man made wine.

Victor Hugo

ACKNOWLEDGEMENTS

We gratefully acknowledge permission to reprint extracts of copyright material in this book from the following authors, publishers and executors:

Extract from *On Drink* by Kingsley Amis, copyright ©1972 Kingsley Amis. Reprinted by kind permission of Jonathan Clowes, Ltd, London, on behalf of Kingsley Amis.

Illustrations

P17	Courtesy of Bloomsbury Auction House
P21	Provided by Pommery Champagne
P33	Christie's Images Ltd 2005
P39	Courtesy of Bloomsbury Auction House
P47	Courtesy of Bloomsbury Auction House
P78	Courtesy of Bloomsbury Auction House
P105	Courtesy of Hardy's Wine

INDEX

FILL YOUR BOOKSHELF AND YOUR MIND

Poker Wit and Wisdom
By Fiona Jerome and Seth Dickson
From nineteenth-century Mississippi riverboats to Cockney gambling dens and .com
casinos, *Poker Wit and Wisdom* takes a lingering look at the addictive world of poker,
dealing out all the oddities, quirks and stories along the way.
ISBN 1-84525-004-4

Wine Wit and Wisdom
By Maggie Rosen, Fiona Jerome and PJ Harris
A lingering look at the wonderful world of wine, *Wine Wit and Wisdom* blends the
banquets of Bacchus with the grapes of wrath, and the fruitiest flavours with the
correct way to judge a bouquet.
ISBN 1-84525-003-6